Faint Clews & Indirections

Faint Clews & Indirections

Manuscripts of
Walt Whitman *and* His Family

EDITED BY

CLARENCE GOHDES

AND

ROLLO G. SILVER

AMS PRESS, INC.
NEW YORK

AMS PRESS, INC.

New York, N. Y. 10003

1965

To

JOSIAH CHARLES TRENT

1914-1948

SURGEON, HISTORIAN OF MEDICINE,

FRIEND

Preface

THE PRESENT VOLUME contains the previously unpublished manuscripts of Walt Whitman and a selection from the Whitman family letters now in the Trent Collection in the library of Duke University. This collection, presented to the University in 1942 by Dr. and Mrs. Josiah C. Trent in honor of their daughters, has already become known through the publication in 1945 of *Catalogue of the Whitman Collection in the Duke University Library: Being a Part of the Trent Collection*, compiled by Ellen Frances Frey. The materials in the following pages are, like most batches of Whitman's papers, miscellaneous in nature, uneven in literary quality and importance, and in general more likely to prove of interest to the scholar or the collector than to anyone else. They will probably be of greatest service to future biographers of the poet, to whom they indeed provide "faint clews and indirections"—sometimes something more.

Such of the manuscripts as are notes for poems or versions of efforts in verse offer new illustrations of their author's methods of composition. One group of these provides a very rare example of Whitman's slatternly process of fabricating a notable portion of "Song of Myself" and was written, of course, prior to 1855. The prose jottings add details concerning his family, his reading, his friendships, or other interests. Occasionally they correct or amplify the existing information about his life. A few, like the notes on Rousseau or on the *Nibelungenlied*, will help to dispel the lingering illusion that Walt was a kind of uncouth bison, powerful chiefly because of his unfamiliarity with the older literary order.   Others reveal a keen observer of the inequities of modern industrial society.

The letters written by his mother and by other relatives are the most novel material in this book. They afford for the first time a fairly substantial basis for judging the mental abilities of the Whitmans and uncover several skeletons in the family closet. Previous accounts of his humble background have hardly prepared us to learn that because of Walt's preoccupation with his errands of mercy among the soldiers in the Washington hospitals his own elder brother was buried from an insane asylum in a potter's field. Nor have we ever heard before that brother Andrew's wife was a foul slut who took to the streets after the death of her husband. Less shocking but still dismaying is the picture disclosed of brother-in-law Heyde, who could on occasion damn *Leaves of Grass* with a will and later "chisel" its impecunious author out of a few more dollars. But despite the scandals and the poverty, there is manifest in many of these almost illiterate letters the imperishable love of a family for a remarkable son and brother who always passed himself off among them as nothing more than their plain and considerate Walt. The phrenological analysis in the Appendix, it may be added, is the only important description of Whitman that dates before 1855.

A word as to our general methods of procedure may perhaps be helpful. In our headnotes, in italics, we have indicated the pages of Miss Frey's catalogue on which the various manuscripts are described, and we have briefly sketched the nature of their contents. Our footnotes have been restricted to what we consider a necessary minimum, and, usually, we have taken for granted upon the part of the reader a fair knowledge of Whitman's life and works. With the exception of those in the poetical manuscripts, we have recorded in notes only a few of the deletions in the original texts. In no case have we indicated all of the deletions. Such faulty punctuation, misspellings, fragmentary sentences, and incomplete words as appear on the pages are the products of Walt himself or of the members of his family. We have not marked them by the use of the word *sic*, and only sparingly have we added words or letters in brackets. But all bracketed material, it should be said, is contributed by us unless otherwise indicated in a note. If there has been any uncertainty in our minds as to the addition of dates or words or letters, we have added the usual question mark. In a number of the letters, especially those written by Mother Whitman, we have at times undertaken to help clarify reading by leaving more space between sentences or sentence fragments than was allowed in the originals. Certain books which we have cited or referred to frequently we have given abbreviated titles or names—such as *Camden* for the Camden Edition of *The Complete Writings of Walt Whitman* and *Glicksberg* for *Walt Whitman and the Civil War*, edited by Charles I. Glicksberg. An explanatory list of these abbreviations or symbols appears on page 237.

The order in which the manuscripts are printed is based upon the following principles. Those poetical manuscripts which are directly connected with poems in *Leaves of Grass* follow the order of such poems in that book as finally revised by Whitman; others appear at the end of the section. The prose manuscripts are presented in the order of their listing in the Trent Collection catalogue. The letters are in chronological sequence within the sections assigned to their respective authors. In a few cases, especially the letters and notes written to William S. Kennedy and the phrenological analysis, excerpts have already been published, but we have nevertheless supplied the full text.

In acknowledging our debt for help from others we put first the name of Miss Frey, without whose friendly aid we should have been sorely distressed. We are also obliged to her for making the index. In all stages of our work we have been assisted by Alice G. Silver, and for help in solving problems connected with annotation we wish to express our thanks to the following: Mrs. Lewis Chase, Miss Edna Huntington, Miss Mary M. McGuire, Miss Ethylwyn Manning, Miss M. Alice Martin, Miss Madeleine B. Stern, Miss Elizabeth Thorogood, Rufus A. Coleman, Arthur T. Hamlin, Clarence A. Manning, Edward Naumberg, Jr., and Edwin Seaborn.

We wish to express our thanks also to the Duke University Research Council for supplying clerical assistance.

CLARENCE GOHDES
ROLLO G. SILVER

Contents

Faint Clews & Indirections

Poems and Notes for Poems

[PRELIMINARY DRAFTS OF PORTIONS OF "SONG OF MYSELF"]

Trent Collection catalogue, page 3, number 1. The immediately following trial flights or "manuscript doings," as Whitman himself called them, were written prior to the appearance of the 1855 edition of Leaves of Grass *and were pasted beneath other sheets by the poet. They were first discovered by Miss Ellen Frey, of the Duke University Library, when she took apart the pages which Whitman had pasted together. Each of the fragments is canceled by one or more lines drawn vertically through the middle of the page—a printer's method of marking manuscript already set up in type and Whitman's usual reminder to himself that the material thus canceled had been put to use elsewhere. The revisions in the lines vary in number and nature from fragment to fragment, but in general they seem to represent a middle stage between initial composition and the text of the 1855 edition. It is clear that, with one exception, these fragments contain lines which belong to sections 6, 7, and 48 of "Song of Myself," as that poem eventually was arranged; the single exception—herein called "Fragment V"—bears only a tangential connection with the baffling passages on touch which appear in sections 27-30 of that poem. Cut up and pasted under other sheets, four of the six fragments nevertheless reveal their original sequence, and the arrangement given them here is that of the order of the lines or ideas in the published text of the poem. The reader is reminded that the very earliest stages in the evolution of "Song of Myself" appear in Whitman's notebooks for the years 1847-1848.*[1]

[Fragment I]

In the course of the wind'g path through the grass[2]

---

[1] Printed by Emory Holloway in *Uncollected*, II, 63 ff.
[2] This entire line was canceled.

And when once they went far enough to see
   the happiness beyond,[3]
That was the reason no wit or temptation could
   draw them back.[4]
And now it seems the dark, uncut hair of graves:[5]
[T]enderly will I use[6] you, tressy grass,
   breasts of young men—[7]

[Fragment II]

It may be you transpire from the[1]
It may be if I had known them I would have loved
   them.
[I]t may be You sprout from little ones[2] taken
   soon out of their mothers' laps,
And now you yourselves are[3] the mothers' laps.
How can you be so dark?
Are you not from the white heads of the old
   mothers?
Are you not from the colorless beards of old men?
[A]re you not from under the faint red roofs of
   mouths?[4]

---

[3] "they went" is written above the canceled words "spirits go." The word "they," accordingly, refers to the spirits of the dead. This line and the one following represent an emended version of lines 5 and 6 of Fragment IV.

[4] The words "to the body" originally ended this line, but they were later canceled.

[5] This line first read: "[Th]is grass is the dark, uncropped hair of graves."

[6] "use" was substituted for "touch."

[7] The first part of this line was trimmed away and appears at the beginning of Fragment II.

---

[1] "transpire" was substituted for "effuse." The last part of this line appears at the end of Fragment I.

[2] "little ones" was first "dead babes," then "infants," then "young ones."

[3] "are" was substituted for "rest in."

[4] This line originally read: "[A]re you not from pale red tongues and mouths?"

[Fragment III]

O, now I know what you mean!
You do not come out of the roofs of mouths[1]
   for not[hing]
[Y]ou would whisper[2] me what is done to the
   young men,
[A]nd to the old men and the mothers

[Fragment IV]

[A]nd the babes[1] taken soon out of their laps—
When even the cinders they left behind them,[2]
When the cinders and soiled rags they dropped as they
   left us,[3]
Even they continue on, and become new live fire, and plenti-
   ful beautiful clothing.
And when their spirits went far enough go far enog to sus
   the happiness beyond,[4]
That is the reason why no wit or temptation ever lures them
   back to the body.[5]
Yet I cannot say what has become
   of the young and old men,[6]
Nor what has become of the women and children

---

[1] "the roofs of mouths" was substituted for "tongues and mouths."
[2] "whisper" was earlier "tell."

---

[1] "babes" was canceled, but no word appears in the manuscript as a substitute. In the 1855 text Whitman substituted "offspring."
[2] This line was canceled in its entirety.
[3] "cinders" earlier read "parings"; "left us" read "went."
[4] This line was apparently rejected by Whitman, who emended it beyond
the point of clarity, struck out the words "their spirits went far enough" (an
emendation), and drew a ligature mark at the left, indicating that this and
the following line were to be replaced. (For the replacement see lines 2 and
3 of Fragment I.) Apparently, this rejected line originally read: "And that
when once the soul goes into the happiness beyond."
[5] This line earlier read: "And that is the reason why no art or cunng can
lure it back to the cold flesh."
[6] The two lines were first written: "Yet I cannot say, any more than you,
what has become of the young men."

Only I am positive[7] they are alive and well
  somewhere.
Because this grass tells me there is no such thing
  as death,
Or if ever there was, it preceded all,[8]
  and does not wait at the end,
And ceased the moment the first live thing began.
And that noth'g collapses,[9] but all goes onward and outward
And that to die is not what what one supposes.——[10]

  ¶Have you supposed it good to be born?
  I hasten to inform[11] you it is just as good to die, and
    I know it;
  For[12] I take my death with the dying,
  And my birth with the new washed babe[13]

[Fragment V]

  My tongue can never be content with harness
    after this,[1]
    It will not talk in[2] traces,

[7] "positive" originally read "sure enough."
  [8] "preceded all" originally read "stood at the beginning." After the correction "preceded all" Whitman wrote "primitive" but later crossed the word out.
  [9] "collapses" originally read "recedes."
  [10] "one supposes" first read "you supposed."
  [11] "hasten to inform" was substituted for "tell."
  [12] Before the word "For" the words "I know it" were written and later canceled.
  [13] The last four lines doubtless represent a revision of the following, jotted in the 1848 notebook (*Uncollected*, II, 71):
      "Have you supposed it beautiful to be born?
      I tell you I know it is just as beautiful to die;
      For I take my death with the dying
      And my birth with the new-born babe."

  [1] This sentence apparently first read: "My tongue must be content with pap / from this."
  [2] Before "in" the word "mean" was written and canceled.

It gives up the bit, and   any more,[3]
So little a thing as touch has unhaltered
    th[oug]ht[4]

[Fragment VI]

And I have discovered them[1] by night and by
    day:
And every one is signed by His Name:
And I leave them where they are, for I know that
    others will punctually come as long as I live,
And afterward, wherever I go they will be for-
    warded to me[2]

[A Note on the Broad-axe]

*Trent Collection catalogue, page 16, number 39 (2). The
following note, written prior to the appearance of the 1856
edition of* Leaves of Grass, *may well be the germinal idea from
which developed "Song of the Broad-Axe." The manuscript is
canceled by two vertical lines. It is, of course, to be distinguished
from the unusually detailed outline of the poem which Bucke
published in* Notes and Fragments *and which Triggs later included in his "Variorum Readings."[1] Whitman seems to have
jotted down his first thoughts on the broad-axe in the present
manuscript, later expanding and adding to them in the detailed
outline.*

—The Broad-axe—the axe of the headsman
First as the axe of the headsman—and what
    was done with it for a thousand years—then

[3] All of the words in this line except the last two were canceled. They
were, apparently, intended to go at the end of the preceding line.

[4] "a" before "touch" was deleted. Compare this line with the following
from the ecstatic passage on touch in the 1848 notebook (*Uncollected*, II,
72): "One touch of a tug of me has unhaltered all my senses but feeling."

[1] "them" refers to "letters from God dropt in the street" ("Song of Myself," section 48).

[2] This line was canceled.

[1] *Inclusive*, pp. 612-614. The manuscript is now in the Trent Collection.

as the carpenter's broad-axe, and what is
done with that now

[PRELIMINARY DRAFT OF A PORTION OF
"SONG OF THE REDWOOD-TREE"]

*Trent Collection catalogue, page 10, number 24. The present
fragment was first discovered by Miss Ellen Frey, of the Duke
University Library, when she separated two sheets of paper
which Whitman had pasted together and upon one of which he
wrote notes for a never-completed poem on "Calls."[1] The lines
represent a preliminary attempt to write out certain ideas later
used by the poet in the tenth strophe of the first part of "Song
of the Redwood-Tree." There are numerous revisions, and the
whole is canceled by two lines drawn through the middle of
the page.*

    occult deep Volitio[ns]
    You Ye occult, deep V[o]
      litions
    You hidden permanent Determinations National,
      Wills,
      lying
      from
      you shapg, & mould'g These Sta[tes]
      your abysms in Time and Spac[e]
    You that alone continue on, destined to ma[n]y
      a cen[tury] yet any Vistas pr[ob]lems,
      speculations, yet shall justify
    You Purposes, tena[ciously]
      pursued, may-be unconscious to
      yourselves,
    Unswerved by all the vex[atious]
      errors, diverse perturbations of
      surface,

[1] The notes appear in *Camden*, IX, 198-199.

To you in your abysms,[2]
   (returng it from when[ce]
   it came)
And you, to you ye centuries to come—
I dedicate this Book.

[PRELIMINARY DRAFT OF PORTIONS OF "THIS COMPOST"]

Trent Collection catalogue, page 7, number 14. This manu-
script was first discovered by Miss Ellen Frey, of the Duke
University Library, when she separated four leaves from the
pieces of green paper upon which Whitman had pasted them to
provide himself with clean sheets for a list of parts of the hu-
man body used by him in revising "I Sing the Body Electric"
for the 1856 edition.[1] It represents an early draft of portions of
"This Compost," especially part 1, and was apparently written
in 1856. Each page is canceled with a line drawn through the
middle, and the margins at the left have been trimmed.

O Mother, did you think
      there could ever be a time
      when I might not
[I] will withdraw awhile among the
      woods or on
      the prairies, or to my
      lover the sea,
I touch my flesh to the earth as to other and
      am re[2]
How can you be so sweet,
      you growths of
      spring?

[2] Whitman first wrote "To ye," then wrote "you" above the line but did not cancel "ye."

---

[1] The list is published in *Camden*, X, 22-23.

[2] The sheet is torn off so as to mutilate the line. In the final version of the poem the reading is: "I will not touch my flesh to the earth as to other flesh to renew me."

How can you be so
   pure, wholesome you blood of herbs,
   roots, orchards, grain?
Are they[8] not continually putt'g
   diseased corpses in the
   earth?
Are not all continents and islands
   sowed with the dead?
Where have you disposed
   the carcasses of
   the drunkards, gluttons,
   of
    so many generations?
[W]here have you drawn off the
   foul meat that has been
   buried in you so many
   millions of years?
I do not see it in you,
   to-day?
I will run a furrow with
   my plow—I will
   press my spade through the
   sod, and turn the earth out
I think I
   shall expose
   again some of that
   foul meat,
No sweet and perfect bodies
   walk upon it—the
   the sour
   flesh is
[I] swear I can hardly believe

---

[8] A question mark is written above "they."

that the earth is not
pestilential,
[Is] it not worked over and
over with the

ter (all is fu
winds are not infectious

all then, fresh?
[Ar]e the winds really not infectious?
[Is] there no cheat in the
transparent greenwash of
the sea? Is it
safe to
allow it to lave
my naked body? Will it[4]

[ADDITIONAL NOTES FOR "PROUD MUSIC OF THE STORM"]

*Trent Collection catalogue, page 10, number 23. At some
undetermined time after the publication of "Proud Music of the
Storm" in the* Atlantic Monthly *for February, 1868, Whitman
may have read an article on Russia containing information on
musical instruments peculiar to that country. The present
manuscript represents notes and ideas from that source intended
to expand, probably, section 5 of the poem—the section in
which the poet attempted to suggest the varied musical offer-
ings of Europe. However, he neither revised his preliminary
draft nor made use of the material in* Leaves of Grass.

[4] The manuscript ends here. How much Whitman added to these pre-
liminary jottings is evident in the final rendering of the idea:
"What chemistry!
  That the winds are really not infectious,
  That this is no cheat, this transparent green-wash of the sea which is so
    amorous after me,
  That it is safe to allow it to lick my naked body all over with its
    tongues. . . ."

corrections
Proud music of the
   Storm
the cohorn, a wind instrument
made of bark, bound
round with wire
used by the Russian shepherds
& The fishermen on
the Don & the
Wolga

I hear the wild sound of
the cohorn from Russ
shepherds or the
fishermen along the
Don, or those of the
Wolga

preced'g the above
the little
bells of the wooden loshki[1]
—The Russian loshki, the
little bells attached to the
wood

I see
In Siberia
the miners dancing
to
plates of metal
struck by boys, with
iron or wood
The old Russian hunting music,
the band composed
of horns only

[1] *Lozhki*, literally "spoons," also means a kind of castanet used by folk-song singers and itinerant entertainers.

[NOTES FOR A POEM ON MUSIC]

Trent Collection catalogue, page 10, number 22. The follow-
ing manuscript, probably dating from the late sixties, contains
ideas used in "Proud Music of the Storm" and "The Mystic
Trumpeter." It adds another bit of evidence attesting to the
importance of music in the composition of Leaves of Grass, *a*
subject which has been discussed by a large number of com-
mentators.[1]

Theme for piece
poem
An opera
? an opera in a dream
—different singers & characters,
—the suggestions, associations

Some old song? hymn? Rock
me to sleep mother?
? Rock'd on the cradle of the deep?
—With its memories, *associations*
—of where I last heard it,
in Hospital.—
—? some typical appropriate
? *tune,* or ? *hymn*—or ? someth'g
played by the band (? some dirge
or ? opera passage or dead ? march

Calling up the whole
dead of the war
The march in last act of *La Gazza Ladra*[2]
One Stanzas must describe

---

[1] For example, Louise Pound, "Walt Whitman and Italian Music," *Ameri-*
can Mercury, VI, 58-63 (Sept., 1925); Henry S. Canby, *Walt Whitman, an*
American (Boston, 1943), pp. 312-313; and Alice L. Cooke, "Notes on
Whitman's Musical Background," *New England Quarterly,* XIX, 224-235
(June, 1946). For Whitman's own estimate of his knowledge of music, see
Traubel, III, 511. Cf. also pp. 18-19 of the present volume.

[2] An opera by Rossini.

a strong *triumphal*
instrumental & vocal *chorus*
as of *triumphant man*—triumphant
over temptation & all
weakness & ?[3]

[PRELIMINARY DRAFT OF "HANDS ROUND"]

Trent Collection catalogue, page 12, number 29. The manuscript is tattered at the top of the page and shows so many cancellations and emendations that there can be no doubt that its contents represent a preliminary effort. Possibly intended as a song for a political rally—and perhaps revised for the Centennial celebration in 1876—the effort was, so far as we know, never published. One stanza of a revised version of this piece, however, has been printed by Mr. Holloway;[1] and a fragment "Comrades All (Hand-in-hand for once)," reproduced in Furness,[2] seems indirectly connected in idea with it. Whitman was certainly working on the poem in 1876, possibly with the intention of offering it as his contribution to the Centennial celebration. It is of interest as representing, with "O Captain! My Captain!" an effort in rhyme and meter.

Hands Ro[und]

[See!] see! see! where the sun is beaming!
See! see! see! all the bright stars, gleaming!
See by day how the sun is beamg
See by night all the far stars glea[ming]
What the charm of Power unbroken?

---

[3] The idea concerning "One Stanzas" was written on the verso of the manuscript and is canceled with a blue pencil stroke. Whitman frequently, but not invariably, employed this method of marking such notes or ideas as he actually used in a published poem. The idea, of course, is embodied in section 8 of "The Mystic Trumpeter."

[1] *Uncollected*, II, 101.
[2] P. 206.

What the spell of ceaseless token?[3]
? O its hand in hand, & a Union of all
What Columbia's ?friendliest token?[4]
'Tis the hands we take for the Union
    of all
Here's mine—give me thine—for the Union
    of all
What Columbia's friendliest token?
All hands round for the Union all!
Here's mine—give me thine—for the Union all

Stars up above in eternal lustre
Stars of the States in a compact clustre
Clasp'g, hold'g, earthward, heavenward
Circling, moving, roundward & onward
All hands round for the Union all
Here's mine—give me thine—for the Union all

Red, white, blue, to [th]e westward[5]
Red, white, blue, with the breezes wav'g
All combining, fold'g, loving,

Northward, Southward, Westward mov'g
O its all hands round for the Union all[6]
Heres mine—give me thine—for the Union all
clasping, circling earthward, heavenward!
Onward! onward! onward! onward!
Stars for the sky in an eternal lustre

---

[3] This line was first written: "What the Charm of heavens own token?"
Later it was made to read: "What the word of God's own token?"; and
"What ?Columbia's ceaseless token?"; "heavenly" was once substituted for
"heavens." Apparently, "word" was first substituted for "Charm"—and
above it was written "spell." Neither "word" nor "spell" was canceled.
[4] This line originally read: "What Columbia's mystic token?" Whitman
wrote "?friendliest" above "mystic" but did not cancel the latter word.
[5] "to" is written above the word "in," but the latter is not canceled.
[6] First reading of this line: "Union all! O its Union all"; Whitman drew
a line through the first three words but neglected to cancel "its."

Stars for the earth in a compact cluster
Then our hands here we give for the Union all!
O its all hand round—and each for all!

[MISCELLANEOUS POETICAL FRAGMENTS]

Trent Collection catalogue, page 14, number 36; page 15, number 38; page 15, number 37. The following jottings are insignificant bits in prose and verse which Bucke either by design or by oversight neglected to publish in Notes and Fragments. *There is no way of establishing their dates. Each one bears a relationship to one or more of Whitman's published works, but no certain connections have been established by the present editors.*

[Fragment I]

And there a hunter's[1] camp
    of hunters
  out on the Adirondacks[2]
    or by the Saginaw lak[e]

[Fragment II]

to you an inheritance[1]
I enjoin the young men, when my voice that
    cast around for some one
    to? extract the informed poe[ms?]
    and form them
Let year after year[2] inherit this
    charge[3]—Let a hundred poe[ts?]
    inherit it.—

---

[1] "hunter's" was substituted for "lumberers."
[2] "Roamg over," "Camping," "Clim'g the"—all three canceled—preceded "out on the Adirondacks."

---

[1] The manuscript, clipped at the top and torn at the right margin, is canceled by a vertical line. The first line was first written "in the air, with indestructible."
[2] "year after year" was substituted for "as many as will."
[3] "charge" was deleted, but no substitute word was written.

[Fragment III]
vegetable
not wood
very common
not in the room
used as food
solid
not fruit of any tree
grows in the ground[1]

[Fragment IV]
To the English and
the French of Canada—
to the Scotch, the Irish,
the German and the Scandinavian[1]

[1] The entire manuscript, written on the verso of "Poem L'Envoy," is canceled by a vertical line. The whole sounds like one of the riddle attempts common enough in *Leaves of Grass*.

[1] This possibly represents one of the numerous dedications prepared but not used by Whitman.

Prose

[Autobiographical Note]

Trent Collection catalogue, page 18, number 4. When, in 1884, Whitman planned to use the plates of the 1881-1882 edition for a new issue of Leaves of Grass,[1] *he probably also intended to publish a companion volume of prose. This paragraph may well have been conceived as a conclusion for such a book. A later paragraph, strikingly similar in style, appears in the "Additional Note" to the 1887 edition of* Specimen Days in America.

Camden—Phila

April 8, '84—

I have been living here in Camden now for nearly eleven years. Came on from Washington in the summer of '73, after my paralytic-stroke, and the death of my dear mother. Continued for three years in quite a bad way, not strength enough to walk any distance—stomach and head miserable. In '76 began to get better—about that time—went board'g down in the country livg in the open air, as described in the preceding volume. From the fall of '76 to the present writing (April, '84) I have been well enough to go around most of the time, with occasional spells of sickness—one of which, (over two months,) I am just now recover'g from.

Italian Singers in America

Trent Collection catalogue, page 22, number 16. This fragment, written while Whitman edited the Brooklyn Daily Times, *constitutes the beginning of an article inspired by Piccolomini's success in the United States. Whitman's admiration of Alboni*

---

[1] *Furness, p. 230; Barrus, p. 251.*

is well known, and this defense of her popularity is not surprising. The description of her in this fragment is, however, more detailed and more revealing than any of his other references to the singer whom he considered "greatest of them all."[1]

This country now has its steady succession of the best Italian singers, male and female. — We do not think much of Piccolomini, the present "rage."[2]— She is not, in reality, as fine a lyric artist as several of those we have heard, in New York, and about whom there has been no furore. — ¶ The best songstress ever in America was Alboni. — Her voice is a contralto of large compass, high and low — and probably sweeter tones never issued from human lips. The mere sound of that voice was pleasure enough. — All persons appreciated Alboni — the common crowd quite as well as the connoisseurs. — We used to go in the upper tiers of the theatre, (the Broadway,) on the nights of her performance, and remember seeing that part of the auditorium packed full of New York young men, mechanics, "roughs," &c., entirely oblivious of all except Alboni, from the time the great songstress came on the stage, till she left it again. — ¶ Alboni is a fully developed woman, with perfect-shaped feet, arms, and hands. — Some thought her fat — *we* always thought her beautiful. — Her face is regular and pleasant— her forehead low — plentiful black hair, cut short, like a boy's —a slow and graceful style of walk — attitudes of inimitable beauty, and large black eyes. — We have seen her in pathetic scenes, (as in Norma plann'g the death of her children,) with real tears, like rain, coursing each other down her cheeks.[3] — Alboni is now in Paris, singing at the Grand Opera there.—

---

[1] *Bucke*, p. 29.
[2] Marietta Piccolomini came to the United States in 1858 (*Grove's Dictionary of Music and Musicians*, ed. H. C. Colles, New York, 1938, IV, 176).
[3] "Such are the things, indeed, I lay away with my life's rare and blessed

[Notes on the "Nibelungenlied"]

Trent Collection catalogue, pages 23, 33, numbers 20, 18. The following notes on and translation from the Nibelungenlied *may be the "running sketch" which is mentioned, but not printed, in* Notes and Fragments.[1] *As to its source we can say nothing except that it bears little resemblance to the discussion of and translation from the poem in Joseph Gostwick's* German Literature.[2] *Whitman himself once admitted that "Only experts in antique German can get along with the Niebelungen,"[3] and we may be sure that Walt was no expert.*

I

Our own account of this poem, "the German Iliad," being but a fragment, and more intended to furnish the reader, in one or two specimens, a glimpse of the old verses, by a free translation of them, we refer those who desire complete resumé of the Nibelungen, to Carlyle's essay of that name — to which, however, we are *not* indebted for our own article in any particular. — The translations we give are original in this article. —

Like all the productions of the earlier northern bards, German or Scandinavian, the poem is not subjective, but eminently objective. — It gives definite characters, good or bad — it relates what is done or said. — All is narrative; no sentiment, or reflection, or corollary.— ¶ We have said that the spinal connection of the piece is Pagan; yet, as we have it, a clumsy attempt is made to Christianize many of the characters. — The knights go to mass; and there is in general, the same change as that attempted with some of the

bits of hours . . . or Alboni in the children's scene in 'Norma'" (*Camden*, IV, 292). In 1891 Whitman still remembered these "real tears" and spoke of them to Wallace (J. Johnston and J. W. Wallace, *Visits to Walt Whitman in 1890-1891*, London [1917], p. 162).

[1] *Camden*, IX, 187.
[2] Joseph Gost[w]ick, *German Literature* (Philadelphia, 1854), pp. 18-31.
[3] *Camden*, IX, 117.

old architecture and sculptures in Rome, by chopping off
a little here and there, and altering the names from Jupiter
or Mars or Minerva to St. Peter and Michael, and the
Virgin Mary. —
Before the vesper hour, lo! a great movement of knights
      in the court-yard,
To engage in a tournament, for the royal pastime. —

Looking on, among the rest, there sat the two wealthy
      queens,
And talked of the heroes worthy of praise.

Then said the beautiful Queen Kriemhilde,
"My husband is the most noble, and by right this king-
      dom, and the rule of it, is his."

Then said the lady Brunhilde, "Nay,
The King, your brother, is most noble — If none were
      living but you and your man,
Then what you say might be — but not while Gunther
      lives."

First went the queen to Hagen, and, looking upon him with
      hatred,
"Restore," said she, "before it is too late, my Nibelungen
      treasure,
Then Gunther and yourself may return to your own coun-
      try."

Then out spoke Hagen, perfectly fearless,
"It is in vain, for I have sworn the treasure shall remain
      buried,
As long as one of Gunther's royal family is alive;
Therefore ask me no more — but do with me what you will."

Then turning to a follower, Kriemhilde commanded him

To go to the cell where Gunther was imprisoned, and dispatch him, and bring the head thither.

Soon Hagen, with horror, with distress in his heart,
Saw the servant appear, with the bloody head of Kriemhilde's brother.

He looked at it a moment, and then with stern resolution, to the queen
"Gunther," said he, "is dead — and Gernot and Giselher, thy brothers all, are dead,
And I shall soon follow them — yet, she-wolf,
I tell you not the hiding-place of the gold and gems."
"So be it, then," said Kriemhilde, "one useful thing, at any rate, you have restored to me,
The sword, the weapon of my noble Seigfried."

With that, she drew Seigfried's sword from the scabbard,
And struck off the hero's head with her own hands,
And Etzel cried aloud in horror, to see what was done.

And at the same time, ancient Hildebrand, springing to his feet,
Exclaimed, in frenzy, "Shall such a warrior fall by the hand of a woman?
Then thus I revenge him!"

And swiftly drawing a dagger, he smote the queen in the side,
And Kriemhilde fell, dying, and her kinspeople gathered round her.

Without avail, therefore, was shed the blood of many valiant princes, and their followers
And over the lost and the dead, Dietrich and Etzel, left alone, lamented.

Thus love doth evermore bring dole and sorrow,
And thus ends the Song of the Nibelungen. —

II

The Nibelungen

vast passions of man, with play of heat & cold & storm, like undercurrents, or volcanos, or stormy seas.

WANTS

Trent Collection catalogue, page 24, number 26. Although the following incomplete manuscript possesses the characteristics of a final draft, no printed appearance has been established. It may have comprised one of the unlocated "Plaza Sketches,"[1] it may have been published in a newspaper edited by Whitman, or it may have been intended to be one of the essays he contributed to various journals. Probably written between 1841 and 1860, it contributes an additional vignette of city life to the Whitman corpus. Although its sympathetic attitude toward the newly arrived immigrant is typical and familiar, this essay provides Whitman's most comprehensive treatment of the subject.

Our daily papers, in New York, show that the "wants" of the human race, hereabout, are by no means those few which philosophers have long been in the habit of recommending. — Every morn'g, there they appear — stretched columns of them — of one general character, and stereotyped phrase — but still with a certain variety that marks the difference of nation, taste, or circumstance. —

Life, to both poor and rich, in great cities, is an excitement and a struggle! — Those of our readers, in the country, who jog along their solid, easy way, and are not in danger of falling on slippery places, know very little of the shifts and frequent desperations of the existence of the poor in cities — which go far to counterbalance the supreme advantages that, (reasoners may say what they like,) make the city so attractive and fascinating.

[1] *New York Dissected*, ed. Emory Holloway and Ralph Adimari (New York, 1936), pp. 227-228.

These "wants" in the news papers are illustrative of the precarious nature of employment and existence here. — The merchants and prosperous mechanics do not appear in their columns — Happily, as to the latter class, in this country, work is not yet so hard to get, or employers at present so lordly, as to make it necessary for the carpenter or mason to run around and look to intermediate agencies for a situation. — And among the commercial part of the community, there is a prejudice against filling even a subordinate clerkship through the means of the "want" column, or Intelligence office. —

The vast majority of those who have to do with the "Wants" department, are, domestic servants who need places, and mistresses who need "help." — Most of the females of the former class are Irish women and girls. — Generally, when they come to the office with their little advertisements they appear decently dressed, some indeed with quite costly attire—a large proportion having been to service, and many of them left of their own accord.—They are stout, square shouldered women, with the well-known Milesian features.—Not a few of them are really good looking; although, as a general thing, the best part of their countenances is an expression of patience, honesty, and good nature.

At the office of the Irish Emigrant Society, may be seen a somewhat different class, too short of cash to pay even for a "want" advertisement; seeking also domestic employment. — They are females "just from Ireland." — Hot as the day may be, any time from June to August, many of them will be sweltering in thick woolen cloaks or shawls; and the whole crowd standing shoulder to shoulder, with red faces, and much panting. — In dress, the substantial is altogether ahead of the graceful, or the seasonable. — Their feet have thick, well nailed, shoes, evidently made to last — the very extreme, against the smart patent leather, delicate soled article, which even our hardy young city workingmen now usually wear in summer. — The bonnets of the women are stout Leghorn, well used by their thrifty mothers or grandmothers, in some cases — and therefore, as may be supposed, without much pretension to style. —

Although, in looking over the miscellaneous collection at the office of the Irish Emigrant Society, a stupid and stultified face may now and then be seen, yet the general run is that of persons of fair natural capacity, although brought up under circumstances that render the traits and usages of intelligent life in the city, at first altogether strange to them. —

At any rate, we never look upon one of these collections of poor creatures, without feelings of sympathy and a devout hope that they may have good luck. — Born in a land, which furnishes to modern times the most appaling instance of how partial and bad government must at last result in wide-spread individual ruin, — — portions of the men and women of that land literally starving to death every year — the immense product of their naturally fertile island, monopolized in the hands of a few, and mostly sent to foreign markets, while they emaciate and die — wages at the lowest figure, and employment hard to be had at that — all the honorable places and civil and religious berths occupied by their tyrants — the numerous passionate struggles they have made for relief, at last tacitly given up in despair — with a sort of horrid contentment under the despotism, insult, poverty and starvation that seem to be their destined fate for ever — how can one help feeling a deep sympathy for these poor men and women, ignorant and awkward as they are?—

¶ Then, did you ever notice, the Intelligence offices, scattered about the city? — Those illustrate the "wants" advertised in the papers. — Sometimes, the low basement rooms will be crowded with Irish girls, seated around on long benches, and holding their linen handkerchiefs and fans in their hands. — Some of them are dressed in real fashion, and, when they go out, will draw on their kid gloves and hoist their parasols. — Yes, a close jam of stalwart female humanity, our eyes often catch in those basements, as we pass. — There they are, perpetually stand'g or seated in that way, waiting for some master or mistress to come along and give them a "call." — Probably, also, many of them dress up and go to the Intelligence Office, from motives like those of the fashionable lady who dawdles a morning through the shops and pavement of Broadway. — To the Irish girl, out of a situation, the Intelligence Office is a place of public seeing and being seen. — She makes acquaintance with many Bridgets and Bettys; and notes are compared, and much interesting kitchen news passed from mouth to ear.—

You will notice, at these offices, hardly any Americans; probably none. — At the places we have beheld in our daily walks, we do not yet remember seeing a single American, of either sex. — The same fact applies generally to the "want" columns.—Indeed, there is something utterly repugnant, in the American character, to the station of a servant. — The nearest we ever came to being in danger from a fight, was, one unfortunate day when we accompanied a newly arrived Swiss gentleman, who had resided some time in England, to dine at one of the New York Fulton street eating houses. — A good looking, democratic, young American, in his shirt sleeves, was rather peremptorily accosted by our Swiss friend, as "Waiter." — The young chap's face turned as red as fire, and he was ready for a scrimmage in a moment. —

Around the doors of the larger intelligence offices, stand and lounge the lads and men who wish work. — They are Irish and English, mostly. — Every well dressed passer, who comes along, is examined by their eyes, with an anxious, appealing sort of look. — The English have ruddy healthy faces, and their square shoulders and large arms look the right sort for labor. — We should think these chaps invaluable upon well conducted farms. They are evidently intelligent, and of a sort who would take pride in doing their work well. —

The Irish boys are ready for anything — but mostly prefer, what indeed they are at first best fitted for, to wield the pickaxe or the spade. — They will generally make a florid description of their capacities, by no means doing injustice to themselves, and winding up with a strong appeal to your personal benevolence, and the special virtue of giv'g them the preference. —

The Englishman, on the contrary, is a man of few words, and rarely claims more than he deserves. — Nor does he press himself upon you.—

Now and then, should you be looking at the scenes in one of these offices, you will see a mistress come after a servant. — Perhaps she is the keeper of a boarding house — a place, by the by where the servants are apt to get plenty of hard work and rough usage. — Her cold eye ranges over the whole crow[d and] at once rejects all the good-l[ooking] girls. — There is always tro[uble at a] boarding house where [there ha]ppen[s to] be a plump, handsome Biddy. — It is very strange.—

The good lady inquires and examines, and ponders and looks sharp. — She thinks well of this one's broad shoulders, but fears that she may be a trifle too fond of whiskey: isn't that the inference from her face? — In the mean time, the poor girls are quite in a state of excitement and emulation; — until the successful competitor marches off with her new mistress as proud as a peacock. —

All these girls, likely, have some friend — some cousin, aunt, or one "whose mother lived near, in the old country" — in whose domicile they are furnished with a shelter, while waiting to get a place. — The kindness of the Irish to each other, of which this is one specimen, puts to the

[COMMENTS ON EMERSON]

Trent Collection catalogue, page 25, number 31. The following rough note contains the basic and most definite statement of Whitman's later opinion of Emerson. It may be observed here that while Whitman put into print occasional remarks mildly critical of his contemporaries, his most penetrating and most severe opinions were often jotted in his notebooks or delivered in personal conversation.

His idea of God (as in the oversoul)[1] is not the modern Scientific idea, now rapidly advancing, far more sublime & resplendent, and reflect'g a dazzl'g light upon Democracy, its twin, but the old old Oriental idea of God, taken up by the Ecclesiasticism of the middle ages, and still continued by the fossil churches of the present day
he has a large substrata of Greek and Latin and also of English — with some German and other —but says little of America, and it not only plays no important figure in his writings as a whole, but hardly appears there

☞ It is certain that the time comes when all merely intellectual writ'g, however fine, has been passed beyond, and ceases to attract or nourish.

---

[1] "is beautiful & tender & orthodox, but" (*deleted*).

Emerson — the poems

— it is all crystal, all a glassy clear stream of thought dis-
tilled, — — we want — not a bit of Homeric, Shakespearean
Rabelaisian red blood, heat, brawn, animality as in

[EXCHANGE OF PRISONERS]

Trent Collection catalogue, page 26, number 34. The follow-
ing three fragments are typical memoranda dealing with the
exchange of prisoners during the Civil War. The poet's in-
terest in the problem was enhanced by the fact that his brother
George was captured on September 30, 1864, and held a
prisoner for five months. The second fragment is a canceled
note supplementing the account of Whitman's efforts to secure
his brother's release.[1]

I

It is generally believed in Washington that the President is in favor of a general exchange, but has been for the
past year overruled by the head of the war Department &
others.[2] The consequences are well known to all who mix
much with the people & the soldiers; the administration
has already established a name for bad faith which will tell
for years to come, and the army is far more deeply incensed
than appears on the surface.

Their blood is on our
own heads[3]

Another side to the exchange

[1] *Glicksberg*, pp. 180-181.
[2] Cf. "Under the President (whose humane, conscientious and fatherly
heart, I have abiding faith in,) the control of exchange has remained with
the Secretary of War, and also with such personages as Major General Butler
and Major General Hitchcock" (*ibid.*, p. 179).
[3] Cf. "In my opinion, the anguish and death of these ten to fifteen
thousand American young men . . . rests mainly upon the heads of members
of our own government" (*ibid.*, p. 180).

II

America," Star spangled Ranner," "Fight for the
Union," &c. —

————————

day and night monotonous — same th'g day after day
and night after night —

Visitors — some visitor — *Sundays,* crowd in front, lookg up
at the windows

————————

Release heard of release 18th

————————

Left 19th Feb. at 5 in the morn'g — marched
down to the tug boat, — (4 secesh
officers in charge — no guard)
mean *Wm Alison,* 380 privates and 20
officers — started from 8 — come
down the *James river* within 10 miles
of Newport News — at noon barrel of
crackers opened — and meat — sang
away the night aboard the boat with
patriot songs (men on deck &c sitt'g
in like slave ship)

transferred to the *Express,* and came down to Fort
Monroe, arriv'g on the 20th at 10 a. m

III

Ideas of prison life — the idea of a sad, degraded, òr altogether unhappy life is *all wrong* — the men were generally in good spirits — nobody shirked his duties — all behaved manly, and as to union sentiment it was stronger than
ever — the life was quite happy, and all the men returned
healthy and fat —[1] *Wounded* and *dying* — there would be
some sick, and of course deaths would occur every day

[1] Cf. "An indescribable meanness, tyranny, aggravating course of insults,
almost incredible—was evidently the rule of treatment through all the southern

Hospital — Lewis Francis, Co. G. 14th (taken at Bull Run Manassas had 14 bayonet wounds in him) fought savage — (released 4 weeks since and is now in hospital in Washington — *will get well*) perhaps 200 in the 3 hospitals — *union* Virginia *prisoners* — these are the most unhappy spirited of all — one man actually died from lice

[THE POET]

Trent Collection catalogue, pages 27, 35, numbers 38, 27. Whitman himself canceled a portion of these notes comparing the singer and the poet, but enough of the text is decipherable to warrant printing. These notes, apparently written before 1855, may have been memoranda for the Preface to the first edition of Leaves of Grass. *Some of the ideas and phrases appear in "Song of the Answerer."*

I

The singers are welcome   most   The singers do not live long — only the poet lives long. — The singers are   and in most ages plentiful;[1] but vast and rare is the day, and divine is the place, that brings forth a poet. — Not every century nor every five centuries contains such a day, nor does every nation hold such a place. (names) These may have ostensible names, — but the name of each of them is one of the singers. — The name of poet is reserved till it is taken by[2]

---

military prisons" (*Camden*, IV, 121). Mr. Glicksberg, who summarized this fragment (p. 179 n.), has very properly remarked upon Whitman's contradicting himself.

[1] The paragraph on Milton which appears in section 30 of Part III of *Notes and Fragments* (*Camden*, X, 8) has been superscribed on this part of the manuscript. In the transcription, Bucke omitted the following which appears at the top: "(Horace & Byron."

[2] In a column parallel to this text, Whitman listed the following: "Poet, bard, minstrel Songster and Songstress Rhymester Versifyer jongleur troubadour Singer mystic-singer, ballad-singer prose-singer froth-singer thrift-singer moral-singer song-singer droll-singer fable-singer love-singer wisdom-singer sea-singer wit-singer passion-singer parlor-singer echo-singer golden-singer silver-singer law-singer head-singer heart-singer."

II

undeniable might — These are some of the varieties of singers:

It is the greatest　　glory and extract known so　　of things, but and the human race. —

?

What always indicates the poet though he may be absorbed even in countries for long portions of time and in the crowd of the pleasant ever rising company of singers. — The singers are the hours or minutes of the light or of the darkness, but the poet is the perfect light and darkness.—[1]

[The Bible]

Trent Collection catalogue, page 28, number 40. This passage contains the nucleus of a thought which was eventually incorporated in "The Bible as Poetry."[1]

Theological inferences once thought orthodox may be demolished by the scientific and historical inquiries of our times, but the collect of the Bible, as a traditional poem various in its sources and times, still remains perhaps the most instructive. suggestive. in the highest sense even artistic. memorial of the past.[2] To the poet, in my opinion it surpasses all else

[Notes on a Poet]

Trent Collection catalogue, page 31, number 9. A fragment, probably about Tennyson, which Whitman may have discarded

---

[1] After partially erasing this manuscript, Whitman used the paper for notes which appear in *Camden*, IX, 230. Two newspaper clippings were pasted next to the notes.

[1] *Camden*, VI, 104-109.

[2] Cf. "If the time ever comes when iconoclasm does its extremest in one direction against the Books of the Bible in its present form, the collection must still survive in another, and dominate just as much as hitherto, or more than hitherto, through its divine and primal poetic structure" (*ibid.*, VI, 109).

*in favor of a similar passage which appears in "Poetry To-Day
in America."*[1]

?But Though so loving, so singing, so dwelling on the
past — celebrating it, *at its best* & its personalities in their
best full as much as Walter Scott, (whom Jefferson accused
of throw'g a false glamour of courage, courtesy, high-man-
ners romance, deference to ladies, &c. in his pictures of
Feudalism, and quite leaving out the meanness, superstition
tyranny, brutal outrages, hoggish greediness & contempt of
life and right that made up four fifths of feudalism) yet
this poet is of singularly current and contemporary spirit.

[NOTES ON ROUSSEAU]

*Trent Collection catalogue, page 32, number 15. The existence,
in the Bucke Collection, of this manuscript translation of Rousseau's* Contrat Social *was first noted by Bliss Perry.*[1] *Furness,
in 1929, printed three extracts from Whitman's marginalia,*[2]
but the complete text has never been available.

*The present editors have not been able to identify Whit-
man's source, but they print the text with the hope that someone else may eventually ascertain the identity of the original
translator.*[3]

The Social Contract, Or, Principles of Right.
Foederis Aequas
Dicamus leges   Virgil, Æneid, II, 324.

Preface, to the First Edition

This little Treatise is extracted from a more extensive
work, undertaken without consulting my resources, and long

---

[1] *Camden*, V, 209.

[1] *Perry*, p. 52.

[2] Clifton Joseph Furness, "Walt Whitman's Politics," *American Mercury*,
XVI, 465-466 (April, 1929).

[3] For a discussion of Whitman and Rousseau, see *Perry*, pp. 277-280.

since abandoned. — The follow'g comprises the greater part of the different fragments which had been written, and which seemed to me best worthy; all else destroyed. —

(I.) Montesquieu has only spoken of positive laws, leav'g his splendid structure incomplete; but we must go to the very source of these laws, to trace the origin of this primitive implied or expressed Covenant which binds all societies together. — The *Contrat Social* has appeared; this forms the portico of the temple, and the first chapter of *L'Esprit des lois.* — We may say in truth of this author — "The Human Race had Lost its Title Deeds — Jean Jaques has found Them." (*Note by Brissard.*)

Rousseau has given the substance of his *Contrat Social* in the fifth book of *Emile*, where traveling is discussed; and another abstract is given in Lettres de la Montagne, (letter Sixth)

Book First.

I wish to inquire whether, tak'g men as they are, and laws as they may be made, some just rule of administration may not be established, in the civil order. — In this research it will be my constant endeavor to ally that which the right permits; with that which policy prescribes, that justice and interest may not be divided. —

I begin without expatiat'g. — I may be asked Who I am — a prince? a lawgiver? — No, neither; and therefore it is I write. —[4]

Chapter First, — Subject

Man is born free, yet he is everywhere in fetters. — He who fancies himself the master of others is only more enslaved than they. — Whence this anomaly? — I know not its cause. — What can legalize it? — I think I can answer. Did I only consider force, and the results arising from it,

[4] "Born a citizen of a free state, and member of its sovereignty" (deleted).

I should say: So long as a nation is constrained to obey, and does obey, it acts well; So soon as it is able to throw off the yoke, and does throw it off, it acts still better; — for it regains its liberty by the same right which deprived it of liberty. For all this, social order is a sacred right upon which all others are based. — This right, however, originates not in nature, but is founded on covenants. — Now to investigate those covenants.

Chapter 2d.

The first Societies.

Family organization is the oldest society and the only natural one. — Yet children only remain subject to the father, while they need his care. Afterward both father and children resume their independence; each is free from the other. — If they still remain united it is because they voluntarily elect to do so. — This common liberty is a consequence of the nature of man. — His first law is that of watchg over his own preservation. — Subsequently, the chief is the symbol of the father, — the people, of the children; and all be'g born free and equal, none can alienate their liberty except for their own interests. — The sole difference is, that in the family the love of the father for the children compensates him for the cares he bestows, (orig.? — Is it not also that the like care was aforetime bestowed upon him — and now he only pays?) — while, in the State the Ruler is compensated by the honor and profit of rul'g. —
?

Grotius denies that all human rights can be established in favor of the governed, citing slavery as an example. — His constant manner of reasoning is to establish the *right* by the deed. (1) A more logical method may be used — but less favorable to tyrants. —

(1.) The ablest researches into public rights often simply consist of the history of past abuses, and we bewilder ourselves to no purpose when we take the pains to study them deeply. — (*Traite des Interests, France*; Marquis Argenson.) — This is precisely what Grotius has done. —

It is doubtful, accord'g to Grotius, whether the human race belongs to a hundred men, or these hundred men belong to the human race; but he seems inclined to the first opinion. — This is also the sentiment of Hobbes. — See the human species thus divided into herds of cattle, each hav'g its chief, who guards but to devour it. — As a shepherd is by nature superior to his flock, so the human shepherds. — Thus reasoned the Emperor Caligula, accord'g to Philon, proving plausibly enough that the kings were gods, or the people beasts. —

The philosophy of Caligula is revived in that of Hobbes and Grotius. — Aristotle had said, before them all, that men are not equal by nature, but that some were born for slavery, and some for dominion. — Aristotle was right, but he mistook the effect for the cause. Every man that is born in slavery is born for slavery; nothing is more certain. — Slaves lose everything in their fetters; even to the desire of quitt'g them; they love their servitude, as the companions of Ulysses loved their brutishness. If there are slaves by nature, it is because there have been slaves against nature. — Force made the first slavery; cowardice has perpetuated it.

I have said noth'g of King Adam, or the Emperor Noah, the father of the three great monarchs who divided the universe, like the children of Saturn, whom we seem to recognize in them. —

Chapter 3d

The Right of the Strongest

The strongest man can never be strong enough to be always

master, unless he transforms force into right, and obedience into duty. — From this arises the right of the strongest, a right which is seemingly claimed in irony, but really laid down as a principle.— But will they not define this word for us? — Force is a physical power; I cannot see what morality can result from its effects. — To yield to force is an act of necessity, not will. — At the most it is an act of prudence. — In what sense can this be a duty? —

Let us assume this pretended right for a moment. — Noth'g but inexplicable nonsense results from it; as the effect changes with the cause, and every force which surmounts the first one, succeeds in right. — So long as we can disobey successfully, we do so lawfully: and, if the strongest is in the right, the only point is to prove who may be the strongest. Of what avail is a right which perishes when force ceases? — If we must obey by force, of what need is duty?

"Submit yourselves to the higher powers." If this means, yield to force, the precept is a good one, but superfluous. — I answer that it will never be violated. — All power comes from God, but all sickness comes from Him also. — Are we therefore to conclude that we are forbidden to call the physician? — When a robber surprises me in a forest, I must surrender my purse to force, — but when I can regain it, am I obliged by conscience to give it to him?

We admit then, that force does not constitute right, and that we are only obliged to obey the legitimate powers. — My first question returns.

Chapter 4th.

Since no man possesses a natural authority over his fellows, and since force does not produce any right, covenants therefore remain as the basis of all legitimate authority among men.

"If a private citizen," says Grotius, "has a right to alienate and cede himself as a slave to a master, why have not a whole nation an equal right?" There are equivocal words here, but we will confine ourselves to *alienate*—that is *to give, or sell.*— x x x x

But if each individual could alienate himself, he could not alienate his children, and theirs, and theirs. —

(that's the strongest point.)

x x x x x x x

(This chapter is to prove that the *right* of Slavery, either through cession, victory, sparing life, or what not, is *null.*—) — He says "The words *Slavery* and *right* are contradictory, each excludes the other."

Chapter Fifth

We must always refer to a first Convention. — Should I grant all the positions which I have just refuted, the advocates of despotism would not be benefited thereby — there will ever be a wide difference between subduing a multitude, and governing a nation. Uncivilized enslaved men and their masters, I do not regard as chief and nation — the interest of one be'g opposed to that of the other, there is no commonwealth. —

x x x x

Chapter Sixth

The Social Compact.

I will suppose that men have reached that crisis where the difficulties that threaten their preservation in a state of nature, exceed their resources in that state. They perish then unless they improve that state. Now men cannot create new forces, but they can unite and direct those which already exist — they can associate, under a representative head, or several heads.—

This union involves all, — yet how can each pledge his strength and liberty, without injur'g his interests? x x x

Given: To find a system of association which shall defend and protect with the whole common force the person and property of each associate, and by which every member, while uniting with all, shall be subject only to himself, thus remain'g as free as before the union. — This is the organic problem, the solution of which is given by the Social Contract. —

    x   x   x

The articles of this Contract are so precisely worded that they cannot be modified. — When analyzed, they reduce themselves to a single point, *The entire alienation of each associate member, with all his rights, to the whole community.* —

    ☞   (?)

    x   x   x   x

Chapter Sixth
The Sovereign power

Orig. W. W.   (In short, the whole of this *Contrat Social*, goes to prove, (1760 - '70) that the true government, and of course the only one for men of sense, is that of *a compact* where laws are administered for justice, equal rights, and *inherent liberty* — as opposed to all the continental European, (especially French) ideas of Government —

Chap. 8th

— This transition from the state of nature to the civil state, produces a remarkable change in man by substituting in his conduct justice for instinct — (*orig* W. W. — What is it then, but instinct, ? — cultivated instinct?) and by giving morality to his actions — It is first at this point that, the voice of duty succeed'g to physical impulse, and right to appetite, the man who until now had regarded no being but himself, is brought to act upon other principles, and consult his reason before listen'g to his inclinations.

Although in this state he yields some of his natural advantages, he gains others, more important — and his faculties exercise and develope themselves, his ideas become enlarged, his sentiments ennobled, and his whole being is elevated to such a degree, that although abuses of this new condition may often degrade him beneath the state which he has quitted, he should unceasingly bless the happy moment which rescued him from it, — and which, from a stupid and insignificant animal, created an intelligent being and a man!

Let us reduce this balance of advantages to terms easy of comparison.—Man's *loss* by the social contract is his natural liberty, and an unlimited right to all that he may have the power to wrest or acquire — His *gain* is civil liberty, and protection in the ownership of what he earns or possesses. —

x   x   x

We may also add, as gain, *moral liberty* which alone renders man truly master of himself — for *obedience to lower appetites* is *slavery*

Chapter *Ninth*

Real Estate.

orig.
W.W.   (— Where Rousseau is yet undeveloped is, in not realizing that the *individual* man or woman is the head and ideal, and the State, City, Governmt, or what not, is a servant, subordinate, — with noth'g sacred about it — noth'g in a Judge or Court either — But all sacredness is in the

individual, — and the other, at most, is but a reflection of the individual's.)

x   x

xx Every man has a natural right to all that is necessary to him (*orig* W. W. — Yes but he must go out, where no one has planted stakes before him. — Also, all wealth, however large is inviolable, being the result of previous ? ? — and because society and individual interests are more benefitted by leav'g it inviolable than by tak'g any from excessive wealth and giv'g it to —whom? — to the poor? (Singularly some of the most important provisions of the specific laws of the Public Lands of the United States, are taken word for word, and idea for idea, from Rousseau's "Contract."

I shall terminate this book by a remark upon which every social system should be based — namely — That instead of destroying natural equality, the social compact, on the contrary, substitutes a civil and legitimate equality for the physical inequality that nature has caused among men, — and That, however unequal they may be in respect to strength or genius, all become equalized by strength, and by right. —

Note. — Under bad governments, this equality is but seeming and illusory, serving only to maintain the poor in their misery and the rich in their usurpations. — In this case the laws are always advantageous to the possessors, and injurious to non-possessors— from which it follows that the social state can only be beneficial to men when all possess some, but none too much, property. —

orig. — Or rather when all have opened to them an equal
right to the avenues and means of reach'g property.

[MEMORANDA ON THE WHITMAN FAMILY]

Trent Collection catalogue, pages 39-41, numbers 1-4, 6. Under the terms of Whitman's will, Richard Maurice Bucke received one third of Whitman's manuscripts, letters, books, and clip-pings. Most of the manuscripts were later printed in Notes and Fragments, *but those "of an autobiographical character" did not appear in that volume. Bucke preserved them with the vain hope of revising or supplementing his* Walt Whitman. *But some of the following notes were eventually used as source material for the biographical sketch in the Camden edition.[1]*

I

In the Revolution, a squad of British cavalrey, on a raid on their own account, came to Kell Van Velsor's, (mother's father,[2] "Uncle Kell,") then a youth, and went to the barn, and were just tak'g away a very fine young sorrel mare. Amy V. V.[3] and Kell's sisters, prevented him by force for a while from going to interfere, but just as the British soldiers were lead'g the mare out, K. broke away from the women, made a rush, and seized the bridle from the thieves. They drew their sabres, and flourished them round his head, but he was resolute; and demanded to see their authority for press'g his horse. As usual, great courage, will, and coolness, stood him in hand. The swords flourished and flashed around his head —the women were in tears, expect'g he would be killed; but he held on to the mare, and the up-shot of it was, the British rode away without her.

Grandmother Whitman. tells that one day a British quartermaster's deputy, with some attendants, came out to her house, (the old house below the hill,) and ordered her to get ready the parlor and adjoin'g bedroom, for an officer of rank, in a few days. She did so, but the officer never came.

---

[1] *Camden*, IX, xi.
[2] Major Cornelius Van Velsor (1768-1837). A summary of the Whitman genealogy is in *ibid.*, I, xiii-xv.
[3] Naomi Williams Van Velsor, wife of Cornelius.

II

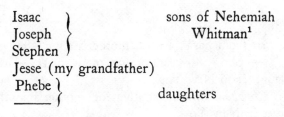

Isaac)
Joseph } sons of Nehemiah
Stephen) Whitman[1]
Jesse (my grandfather)
Phebe }
—— } daughters

Hannah Brush, daughter of Tredwell Brush & ———*Platt*
Her parents died when she was quite young, she was adopted
by her aunt Vashti Platt[2] — This latter must have been
mistress of quite an estate, for grandmother related that she
has seen fourteen little niggers, belonging to the family,
eat'g their supper at even'g, all at once in the kitchen. Tredwell Brush, her brother, died a young man unmarried.

III

Hannah Brush, (my grandmother Whitman) had only one
brother, who died a young man — (the grave-stones from
his grave were among those I saw at the back door.)

——

And only one sister who married —— Scudder, father of
old Tredwel Scudder, (on the South Side.) who was father
of Tredwell, Walter Richard, Wilmot, Hannah & Julia
Scudder

[1] "One of Nehemiah's sons was a lieutenant in Col. Josiah Smith's regiment of the American army. He participated in the disastrous battle of
Brooklyn and there lost his life. In 'The Centenarian's Story,' in *Drum Taps*,
will be found some impersonal account of this portentous event" (*Camden*, I,
xix). However, The National Society of the Sons of the American Revolution possesses no record of a Lt. Whitman in Col. Smith's regiment (letter
from McDonald Miller, Aug. 3, 1946).

[2] The information in this passage was used by Bucke, Harned, and
Traubel (*Camden*, I, xviii-xix).

IV

Portland
avenue

Oct. 29, '62 — Brooklyn
— A visit from Sarah Mead, mother's aunt, (her mother's sister.[1]) — She is 80 years of age, quite smart — lives with her daughter in New York.

Phoebe Pintard, another of mother's aunts, aged 85, lives in New York.

Mrs. Clara Avery, aged about 82, is also living.

Peggy Williams, (another) an old maid died about two years ago.

(The above are four of the eight daughters of Capt. Williams, mothers maternal grandfather)

V

1873. Nov. 20. Camden.

Just rec'd word from N. from mother's aunt, Mrs. Sarah Mead, (born Williams.) She is now in her 92d year, having been born 24th Sept. 1782. On her 91st birth-day, now just past, she rode in a carriage through Central Park, & took great interest & pleasure in the scenes. Her sister, Mrs. Phebe Pintard, died a few years since in N. Y.; must have been nearly a hundred years old.

VI

Mother's family lived only two or three miles from West Hills — on a solitary picturesque road, that wound up from Cold Spring Harbor. — Her father was Major Van Velsor, and her mother's name Naomi Williams.—Capt. Williams and his wife, her parents, fine old couple, exceed'g generous. — I remember them both (my mother's parents)

[1] An obituary of Sarah Williams Mead is in the New York *Times* for April 12, 1878. Accompanying this note are two clippings, signed W. H., containing the reminiscences of Sarah Mead. One clipping bears the following endorsement in Whitman's hand: "death of Aunt Sarah Mead early in April '78 — N. Y. Eve Post Feb 22 '78."

very well. She was a mild, gentle, and sweet tempered woman, fond of children — remarkably generous and hospitable in disposition —a good wife and mother. — In dress she was rather Quakerish. — Her mother's (my great grandmother's) maiden name was Mary Woolley, and her father, Capt. Williams, was owner of a vessel that sailed between New York and Florida.[1]

Major Van Velsor was a good specimen of a hearty, solid, fat old gentleman, on good terms with the world, and who liked his ease. — For over forty years, he drove a stage and market wagon from his farm to Brooklyn ferry, where he used to put up at Smith & Wood's old tavern on the west side of the street, near Fulton ferry. — He was wonderfully regular in these weekly trips; and in those old fashioned times, people could almost tell the time of day, by his stage passing along the road — so punctual was he. — I have been up and down with him many times: I well remember how sick the smell of the lampblack and oil with which the canvass covering of the stage was painted, would make me. —

After my own grandmother died, in 1826[2] the old man married again[3] — He had a son Alonzo, by this second marriage — now, (Sept. 1850,) in California. He is a good young man, I think, from what I know of him. —He has since returned from California with his "pile," went into business in New York, and died at Newark, N. J. July 22, 1883[4]

tomb stones; for on the old hill, at the native place, among

---

[1] Bucke, Harned, and Traubel used much of this information in *Camden*, I, xx.

[2] Whitman questioned this date, writing ?3 above the 2. According to Bucke, Harned, and Traubel, Naomi W. Van Velsor died in 1826 (*Camden*, I, xiv). See also J. Johnston and J. W. Wallace, *Visits to Walt Whitman in 1890-1891*, p. 124.

[3] "but did not make a very good investment"(*deleted*).

[4] An obituary of Alonzo Van Velsor appears in the Newark *Daily Advertiser* for July 23, 1883.

all the numerous graves, there is not one inscribed grave stone,[5] except Mahala Whitman, and I think I have heard that that was put up at the instance of a young man who was to have been married to her. —

The old house in which my father's grand parents lived, (and their parents before them,) is still partly standing — a ponderous frame; it is now turned into a carriage house and granary.[6] — The largest trees near it, that I remember, appear to have been cut down. —

The Whitmans were among the earliest settlers of that part of Long Island — West Hills, township of Huntington, county of Suffolk, New York. — They must have originally come from some rural district of England — a stalwart, massive, heavy, long-lived race. — They appear to have been always of democratic and heretical tendencies. — Some of them are yet represented by descendants in New England

My father's grandfather was quite a large territorial owner in that part of Long Island, and also on the southern shore of the town. — They all espoused with ardor the side of the "rebellion" in 76. —

I remember when a boy hearing grandmother Whitman tell about the times of the revolutionary war. — The British had full swing over Long Island, and foraged every where, and committed the most horrible excesses —enough to make one's blood boil even to hear of now. — My father's father I never saw. —

VII

Nov. 23d. 62 Portland av.

Jesse Whitman the youngest of the children (my grand-

---

[5] "Fifty or more graves are quite plainly traceable, and as many more decay'd out of all form. . . . My whole family history, with its succession of links, from the first settlement down to date, told here — three centuries concentrate on this sterile acre" (*Camden*, IV, 8-9). Wallace, in 1891, found two legible headstones (Johnston and Wallace, *Visits to Walt Whitman in 1890-1891*, p. 121).

[6] Bucke, Harned, and Traubel mention this in *Camden*, I, xix.

father) had 2 (or ?3) brothers, older than himself, Stephen and Isaac; and one sister, Phebe. — She married Zaire Jarvis, (he lived just west of Babylon, on the South road, in 1840)

Isaac had a son *Jacob Whitman* a carpenter, — of this Jacob him my father learnt his trade — the first part of the time about Huntington West Hills, &c. and the last portion of his apprenticeship, (?about—years) in New York city. —

Jacob Whitman, (above mentioned) worked as a sort of foreman for a Venetian blind maker in New York — who died, and J. W. married the widow, and had two children by her — She died, and then J. W. married her daughter, and by her had quite a brood of children

VIII

Father finished his apprenticeship in New York city, and then worked for some three years there — I have heard him speak of boarding steady for three years in New York in one place. He then went up around the Hills, and South, Long Island, and took contracts at build'g. He was a first rate carpenter, did solid, substantial, conscientious work.[1] I have heard mother say that he would sometimes lay awake all night plann'g out some unusally difficult plan in his building arrangements.[2]

IX

Walter Whitman married Louisa Van Velsor June 8, 1816
Mary E. Whitman & Ansel Van Nostrand, married, Jan. 2, 1840.
Hannah Louisa Whitman & Charles Louis Heyde, married 16th March 1852.[1]

[1] This is the source of the information in *Camden*, I, xvi-xvii.
[2] The verso of this page of the manuscript bears the following canceled words: "Vedder / at Brother Jonathan / office Beekman st. / — ½ past 3 — in the rear."

[1] This manuscript, probably written between 1848 and 1855, contains

Walter Whitman born July 14th 1789. -died July 11th
    1855: aged 66 buried at Evergreen Cemetery
Louisa Van Velsor born Sept. 22, 1795
Jesse Whitman born March 2, 1818.[2]
Walter Whitman Jr. born May 31, 1819
Mary Elizabeth Whitman born Feb. 3, 1821
Hannah Louisa Whitman born Nov. 28, 1823
Infant born March 2d 1825[3]
Andrew Jackson Whitman, born April 7th 1827
George Washington Whitman born Nov. 28th 1829.
Jefferson Whitman, born July 18th 1833
Edward Whitman born August 9th 1835[4]
Infant died Sept. 14, 1825, aged 6 months & 12 days.

Naomi or Amy Williams was daughter of Capt.
Williams and his wife Molly Williams.[5] — Besides two sons,
they had eight daughters, Amy, Sally, Peggy, Hannah,
Clara, Molly[6]

        —They lived in a little house high upon
the hills at Cold Spring. — Aunt Molly, the mother was
easy, good-natured, and inclined to let thgs go.[7] Capt. Williams followed the sea. —

---

three dates which differ from those in a later one. In the Bible which Whit-
man presented to his sister, Mary E. Van Nostrand, in 1878, the date of
Hannah Whitman's marriage appears as April 16, 1852 (Katherine Molinoff,
Some Notes on Whitman's Family [Brooklyn, 1941], p. 7).

  [2] In the Van Nostrand Bible this date is April 2, 1818 (*ibid.*).

  [3] In the Van Nostrand Bible this date is April 12, 1825 (*ibid.*).

  [4] A newspaper announcement of the death of Whitman's father is pasted to
the manuscript at this place.

  [5] According to Bucke, Harned, and Traubel, Naomi Williams was the
daughter of Captain John Williams and Mary Woolley Williams (*Camden*, I,
xx).

  [6] In *Specimen Days*, Whitman wrote that the Williams family consisted
of seven sisters and one brother (*ibid.*, IV, 10).

  [7] According to Whitman's executors, "His wife Mary was easy, good-
natured, and with perhaps a deserved reputation for domestic shiftlessness"
(*ibid.*, I, xx).

[A CARPENTER'S RECORD]

Trent Collection catalogue, page 41, number 7. The following penciled notes appear on the verso of the cover of Jefferson Whitman's "Writing Book." While it has hitherto been assumed that the poet's housebuilding activities were conducted by himself[1] or as assistant to his father,[2] it is now apparent that as late as three years before the publication of Leaves of Grass *Whitman hired out as journeyman carpenter.*

35 Lispenard
Carpenters risk
expires Jan 13th
Jefferson Whitman
Writing Book
Brooklyn

July 31st 1852 — Mr. Scofield[3] owes W. W. for eleven days work

Aug 14 - Inclusive of to-day —(half a day for the week ending Aug 7th) — six days and a half — altogether 17½ days

Aug 21 — Made full week the past week (Scofield owes for 23½ days)

$26.42

[NOTES ON THE KELSEYS]

Trent Collection catalogue, page 41, number 8. Whitman's interest in the Kelsey family, according to the following jottings, continued for several years. He may have preserved this information in order to prepare a tribute to the patriotism of the Kelseys. Yet, curiously enough, young Kelsey's name does not

---

[1] "He afterward built and sold moderate-sized houses" (*Bucke*, p. 24).

[2] "We know also that about this time he assisted his father in housebuilding" (*I Sit and Look Out*, ed. Emory Holloway and Vernolian Schwarz, New York, 1932, p. 8).

[3] The only Scofield listed in the 1851-1852 Brooklyn Directory is Minard S. Scofield, carpenter, Bond c State (letter from Edna Huntington, June 19, 1946).

appear in Specimen Days *although he probably was the fellow in the bed next to Charles Miller.*[1]

(Elan E. Kelsey)[2]   Feb. 24 — 1865
(started from Napoli, Cattaraugus co. N. Y father lives there now, March '65)

      Eugene Kelsey
        co B, 64th N Y Vol.

(aged 17 when enlisted)
by spherical case slug, explosion or(cast iron ball). 13th **Dec.** First Fredericksburgh, leg amputated, on the field — brought to Wash'gton (Armory Square) saw him there dur'g Feb, March, &c 1862[3] — (side of Charly Miller)

ages

32 Peter P.   37th N Y Dead, buried in soldier's bury'g
                ground Fairfax Seminary

29   Martin V — now at Petersburgh, in 179th N.Y. re-enlisted

27   William H in 13th N Y. heavy artillery, re-enlisted

        Heman L   37th served his time out, & is now home married

22   Elan E

20 -   Enos M — in 64th — re-enlisted — taken prison-
                er at Reams's station Nov. '64. &
                has not been heard from since

17 -   Orson — 64th discharged — served his time out
3 years —all pretty well — the above comprises the entire family of sons — went in the war at the commencement

<hr>

[1] *Camden*, IV, 42.

[2] According to the records of the Adjutant General's Office, young Kelsey's name was Elon.

[3] The year was, of course, 1863.

(Post office address
  Elm Creek
    Cattaraugus co
      New York
leaves Wash'gton Feb. 25. '65)
(the husband of one of the daughters, also a soldier, (Sylvester Nichols, 13. N Y heavy artillery) died at Norfolk, in the service.)

is a very good specimen of that useful class. makes the impression on me of materialism, is not given at all to sentiment or any th'g in the way of strong feel'g or aff — a plain, real, practical young man.

[PROPAGANDA]

Trent Collection catalogue, page 43, number 12. Although a search of probable locations has failed to reveal a printed appearance of this note, its completed form suggests that a copy was at least submitted for publication. Written approximately one year before his death, it is one of Whitman's final paragraphs about himself.

24
Feb. 1891
===

In Notes if convenient

Walt Whitman's bad spell, (the *grippe*, combined with chronic bladder and gastric trouble) continues yet gravely. He keeps in harness however. The March *North American Review* has an essay by him.[1] The March *Lippincotts'* has a reminiscence[2] and also some poetical "old age echoes".[3]

[1] "Have We a National Literature?," *North American Review*, CLII, 332-338 (March, 1891).

[2] "Some Personal and Old-Age Memoranda," *Lippincott's Monthy Magazine*, XLVII, 377-381 (March, 1891). "The Old Man Himself. A Postscript" appears on p. 389.

[3] "Old-Age Echoes," *ibid.*, p. 376.

Whitman's little 2d Annex, *"Good-Bye my Fancy,"* is in the printers' hands.   It is intended to complete *Leaves of Grass.*

[The Purpose of "Specimen Days"]

Trent Collection catalogue, page 45, number 20. The follow-
ing statement of the purpose of Specimen Days *may have been*
sent to Bucke as source material for the proposed revision of
his biography. A more detailed and probably earlier version
appears as a footnote to the first paragraph of Specimen Days.[1]

for Dr B's Criticism

— as far as it may be stated The purpose object of *Specimen Days* was to combine & weave in one pattern (for those at all interested in it, or caring to pick it out, and for my own satisfaction,) for it & for me* certain variegated record-threads of my personal experience, young manhood in New York City and Brooklyn, with what I had seen of the Secession War 1861-'5, hospital scenes and interiors, the actual rank and file from all the States, — then — afterward, for four or five years, notes and jottings of simple out-door rural Nature, as playing upon the emotions of a convalescent, a half-paralytic and played upon in return — some of my reflections in the mean time, on literary characters, especially Carlyle — with a "Collect" of various pieces, comments on my time and spirit of the time, especially as in "Democratic Vistas")

— all scooped and swept in together, indeed (like hauling a fish-seine)[2] — some parts and pieces elaborated, stated as I am content to have them — but a great deal of the book crude notes and diary-jottings, personal and perhaps trivial — my purpose being (I suppose) to give glints and glances into[3] actual life-happening

[1] *Camden*, IV, 3-4.
[2] "The *Collect* afterwards gathers up the odds and ends of whatever pieces I can now lay hands on, written at various times past, and swoops all together like fish in a net" (*ibid.*, IV, 4 n.).
[3] "my" (*deleted*).

[WHITMAN AND BLAKE]

*Trent Collection catalogue, page 47, number 28. Whitman's
interest in William Blake was never great. Indeed, in the
Camden edition, Blake is mentioned only once — in a reference
to the "half-mad vision of William Blake."[1] But when Swinburne's* William Blake *appeared in 1868, the final pages were
devoted to a comparison of Blake and Whitman,[2] and the latter,
as usual, attempted to continue the publicity. The following
paragraph, written on stationery of the Attorney-General's
Office, is contemporary with the appearance of Swinburne's
book.*

Of William Blake & Walt Whitman   Both are mystics,
extatics but the difference between them is this — and a vast
difference it is: Blake's visions grow to be the rule, displace
the normal condition, fill the field, spurn this visible, objective life, & seat the subjective spirit on an absolute throne,
wilful & uncontrolled.   But Whitman, though he occasionaly
prances off, takes flight with an abandon & capriciousness of
step or wing, and a rapidity & whirling power, which quite
dizzy the reader in his first attempts to follow, always holds
the mastery over himself, &, even in his most intoxicated
lunges or pirouettes, never once loses control, or even equilib-
rium.   To the pe[rfect] sense, it is evident that he goes off
because he permits himself to do so, while ever the director,
or direct'g principle sits coolly at hand, able to stop the wild
teetotum & reduce it to order, at any a moment.   In Walt
Whitman, escapades of this sort are the exceptions.   The
main character of his poetry is the normal, the universal,
the simple, the eternal platform of the best manly & womanly qualities.

[JOTTINGS FOR 1881]

*Trent Collection catalogue, page 49, number 34. The follow-
ing two rough notes relate to Whitman's second Boston visit*

[1] *Camden,* VII, 16.
[2] Algernon C. Swinburne, *William Blake* (London, 1868), pp. 300-303.

*in 1881. The purpose of this trip, to prepare for the second
Boston edition of* Leaves of Grass, *is summarized in the first
note. The second is a companion-piece to a memorandum written
in the Boston station.*[1] *Two newspaper clippings,*[2] *annotated
with directions for reprinting, accompany these notes and serve
as additional evidence that Whitman planned an article about
his trip.*

I

Sept: '81
Copy of
Leaves of Grass
Set up, cast, & printed
Boston
Aug: 22 - Sept: 29- '1881
at office of
RAND, AVERY & CO.
PRINTERS,
No. 117 Franklin St.
BOSTON.

(1881)

Henry H Clark[3]
    superintendent Book Department

J R Osgood & Co: 211 Tremont st:
    publishers of book

it is to be $2 retail - & I am to
    have 25cts a copy royalty

[1] *Walt Whitman's Diary in Canada*, ed. William Sloane Kennedy (Boston, 1904), pp. 60-62.
[2] "A Poet's Supper to his Printers and Proof-Readers," Boston *Daily Advertiser* for Oct. 17, 1881, and a review of *Leaves of Grass* from the Toledo *Journal* for Jan., 1882.
[3] Additional notes about Clark are in *Furness*, p. 265.

I was in Boston from Aug: 19 to Oct[4]

Dan Rogers - the boy messenger

---

boarding place, Mrs. Moffitt's, Hotel Waterston
8 Bulfinch place[5]

II
N Y Mott Haven
Nov 3 '81

I am writ'g this at Mott Haven station, wait'g for the downward cars — going back to Camden, after an absence of three months. The last twelve days, stopping at the hospitable house of Mr. and Mrs. J H J.[1] here having an easy & restful time.[2] Sent "My Long Island Antecedents" to North American Review.[3] Just read a most live, affectionate, and   criticism on the new L of G. in last Sunday's Boston Herald,[4] by Sylvan.[5]

[WHITMAN ON WHITMAN]
Trent Collection catalogue, page 49, number 36. Another version of the first paragraph appears in Notes and Fragments,[1] *but the second paragraph, not noted by Bucke, contains additional information about the poet's opinion of his own work. For unity, the complete text is printed.*

[4] Whitman left Boston on October 22 (*Walt Whitman's Diary in Canada*, p. 60).

[5] Perry, Kennedy, and even Baxter, who suggested the hotel, refer to it as the Hotel Bulfinch. According to the Boston directory, however, Hotel Waterson is the correct name (*The Boston Directory*, Boston, 1881, p. 1143).

[1] Mr. and Mrs. J. H. Johnston.
[2] The remainder of this paragraph has been canceled.
[3] This article was, evidently, rejected.
[4] "Leaves of Grass," *Sunday Herald* for October 30, 1881.
[5] "Sylvan" was Sylvester Baxter.

[1] *Camden*, IX, 28-29.

Two suggestion points for letter

We have had man in love and war, (perhaps indeed the
most merely natural, universal elements of human lives,
human interest) — man in courts, bowers, castles, dungeons
— man in personal haughtiness, and contests of strength,
as in Homer — or passion crime, jealousy, morbid infatua-
tion, carried to extremes, as in Shakspere — humanity in
divine ravishing tales, always with an indoor atmosphere,
and under artificial and feudal relations.   But never before
have we so thoroughly had Man in the open air, confront-
ing, and a part of, Nature and the seasons, and so squarely
adjusted as one might describe it, to the sun by day, the stars
by night, and affiliated to their own spirit, as in these poems.

He turns Nature, with its *ensembles*, always in human
relations.   It is not only the infinite and relentless Queen,
unspeakably mysterious and separate; it is our Mother,
holding us with undying ties, affections.   Tenderly she gave
us birth — is ever ready for us through life, with health,
with silence, with consolation; tenderly receives us at death.
Then the singular problems of the subjectiveness of Man in
the objectiveness of the Universe — "thou art so near, and
yet so far"[2] — Whitman unhesitatingly grapples with, and
I think solves them as far as they are capable of solution

[TRAVEL NOTES]

Trent Collection catalogue, page 50, numbers 37-38.   During
his three longest journeys (to New Orleans, Denver, and
London, Ontario), Whitman continued his habit of making
copious notes.   The Trent Collection possesses three series of
these notes — one for each journey — each series registering
the poet's impressions of his travels.   Some of these notes were
altered and included in Complete Prose; *all of them, however,*
record Whitman's immediate impressions of new surroundings.

[2] Cf. "He seems so near and yet so far," (Alfred Tennyson, *In Me-*
moriam, London, 1855, p. 146).

I

wooding at night — the 20 deck hand[s] at work briskly
as bees — in going up the river[1] the flat-boat loaded with
wood was attached to the side of our steamer and taken along
with us, until the wood was transferred —

Spectacle of the men lying around in groups on the forward part of the lower deck at night —some asleep some
conversing — glare of the fire upon them — Some emigrants
on their way "up country" — young fellow and his stout
young German wife. — Gruffness of the mate to the boat
hands — (Life, lot, appearance, characteristics, pay, recklessness, premature deaths, etc etc of the western boat-
hands.)

expressions of the mate. — "Step along, bullies!" "Come,
bullies, hop, now! hop now!"

mixture of passengers. — A couple of those re[s]pectable
old gentlemen who are sent to great "Conventions. — Our
two were on the way to Philadelphia. — At the place where
we took one of them up (describe his appearance, his silver
mounted cane etc,) he had about two-score hands to shake,
and as many "good-byes" to utter. —

"Now, Uncle Daniel, you must nominate Clay," said
one. —

"Taylor, Uncle Dan" sang out another

(Had there been time, we should no doubt have had an
argument; but western steamboats, like wind and tide, wait
for no man, on certain occasions, and this was one of them. —
(Describe this old gentleman['s] manner on the boat his
kid gloves.)

The other convention man, seemed to be generally known
too — he was called "Doctor"; wore a white cravat; was

---

[1] Whitman is describing his trip up the Mississippi on his way home in
1848. For notes on the remainder of this journey, see *Uncollected*, II, 78-
79, and *Camden*, VI, 208-216.

deaf, tall, apparently rhumatic, and slep[t] most of the passage — except about meal

Cookery of the boats bad —raw strong coffee — too much grease[2] — haste of the people to get to the table — would rush in and seize their chairs, ready to spring into their places the moment the bell rang. —

Long monotonous stretch of the Mississippi — Planter's dwellings, surrounded with their hamlets of negro huts — groves of negro men women and children in the fields, hoeing the young cotton

our competition, or race, with the "Grand Turk" — continued from day to day.— Deceptiveness of the steamboat officers as to time of starting, etc. —Gallantry toward the females. — Painful effect of the excessive flatness of the country. —

II

the RR we go on (Sept 13 '79) from St Louis to Lawrence)[1] is *the* (northern) *St Louis and Kansas City RR*, 275 miles (from St L to K C) right through the (northern) centre and natural beauty and richness of this great State. Cross'g the Missouri river on the bridge at the pretty town of St Charles, we enter upon the finest soil, show (on a loose, slip-shod scale) trees, beauty, eligibility for tillage of crops, and general look of open air health, picturesqueness that I ever saw, and continue all day on the same enchant'g

nearly three hundred miles —ahead of any thing in Pennsylvania or New York states good as those are

they raise a good deal of tobacco in these counties of Missouri, you see the light greenish-gray leaves pulled and now (Sept 13, '79) in great patches on rows of sticks or frame-

[2] When describing the trip down to New Orleans, Whitman said that "for breakfast, (as at the other meals, too,) the quantity is enormous, and the quality first rate" (*Uncollected*, I, 188).

[1] This series comprises notes written during the Denver trip of 1879.

works, hanging out to dry — looking like leaves of the mullein, familiar to eastern eyes.[2]

Yet, fine as it is, it isn't the finest part of the State. (There a bed of impervious clay and hard pan every where down below on this line, that holds the water —"drowns the land in wet weather, and bakes it in dry," as some one harshly said.) South are some rich counties; but the beauty spots of Missouri are the north-western portions

Missouri
mules (first) oxen, horses —products on the largest scale — everything all varieties and no stint — cattle, wheat, maize, hay, hemp, tobacco, corn wine wool fruits, —

Kansas
—every where products and people and energy and practical ? — every where towns going up, provided or be'g provided with the best, pavements water, gas, parks, police print'g office — everywhere the Railroad, equipped with the best

Wednesday
Sept 17 '79
Topeka Kansas

---

the ride about Topeka[3] (driven by William Muroe) —fine hard smooth roads miles and miles of them —over a flat & unbroken surface, stretchg in every direction as far as the eye could see — the Capitol, (only one fine wing of it, the rest to be) —the Governor — Chief Judge Horton, other Judges

[2] A revised version is in *Camden*, IV, 254.

[3] A comprehensive treatment of Whitman's Kansas visit may be found in Robert R. Hubach, "Walt Whitman in Kansas," *Kansas Historical Quarterly*, X, 150-154 (May, 1941).

abt Sept 20 '79
How inexpressibly magnificent and ample it is! The contrast
—the alternation!   After these easy-peaceful and fertile
prairies of a thousand miles area, corn & wheat & h start up
the grandest mountains of the globe, with many a savage
canon, and cloud pierc'g peaks by hundreds! —and spots of
terror & sublimity Dante and Angelo never knew

going east, after we leave Sterling, Kansas the sun is up
about half an hour— every th'g fresh and beautiful — the
immense area flat as a house floor, visible for 20 miles in
every direction in the clear air.   The grass all autumn yellow and reddish tawny.   Little houses, farms, enclosures,
stacks of hay, dotting the landscape — the prevail'g hue a
rich[4]

III

London — 1880

Then about drinking habits.[1]

My observations and goings around here pretty freely,
indoors and out, note, so far, a singular scarcity of cases of
intemperance; I have seen no drunken man (nor drunken
woman.)—have run across no besotted or low or filthy
quarters of the town either. I should say it was an unusually
temperate city.   Here for a thousand people at the Insane
Asylum, no alcohol-beverage is used — not a pint a week.
The head physician, Dr Bucke, never prescribes it; some of
the assistants at rare intervals.   Dr B. tells me he thinks
it needless, and can get along just as well without it, or even
better, under any circumstances.

[4] The above six lines were canceled.

[1] These notes may have been intended for the Ottawa lecture. In this
lecture, Whitman planned to say, "I shall certainly not only be unable to tell
you anything new, but it may very likely prove that I have only caught surface and present surface impressions" (*Camden*, IX, 25-26).

London Canada June 1880
  for London
Dufferin College
  Huron College for theology
  a good high school

the Savings and Investment Society offers money to farmers
& others at 7 and 7½ per cent, with privilege of paying
interest or principal in instalments
— a good yellow brick, made here is plentiful and cheap
— many fine mansions with gardens, some of exceptional
size and elegance — on Dundas and Richmond —   streets,
the principal rows of shops, offices, banks

— Queen's and Dufferin avenues for fine residences also
Ridout street, old & fine, backing the river
    many handsome churches
— a large and fine Revenue Office building, also Post Office,
also several Bank Buildings, also some large Hotels, the
Tecumseh House
    and many four-story houses in rows, with stores on the
ground story
                    Some of the streets
Queen's avenue,
    very wide either their whole length or in part, and
agreeably parked with grass and trees
    —London stands mainly on high ground in the fork be-
tween the north & south branches of the river (Thames)
over the south fork is Westminster
over the north fork Petersville
    The Thames river winds its twirling and shallow, but
very pretty waters to the   ?   of the main body of the
town, and on the   side are clusters of comfortable houses,
mostly one or two storied, quite democratic, with now and

then a costlier one. I saw on the river several small-sized steamers, neat-looking, hawsered, waiting for passengers, or steaming up or down, with the British colors flying.

Of banks and banking houses there are nine or ten.
some 20 churches
The population is 25,000
There are several lines of horse-railrays. I occasionally saw members of the police patrol, with helmets and white gloves — all I saw were fine-looking young fellows.

—

the pavement question
some concrete

By what I am told London would show finely to my eyes in September, from the great annual fair, when there is a gathering of the farmers and their families, men and women, especially the young people — altogether many thousands, and the streets all alive with them for several days
On this occasion one would get a direct view of the average People, the *humanity* of this part of Canada (the main thing of every country.) By what I am told I am sure this average would please me much, and would be a very high

There are two large and live daily papers here. the *Advertiser* and *Free Press*
the R R's

Hellmuth College superior extensive school for young ladies

the Asylum is the show place of London, it and its handsome grounds being always visited by journeyers.
The land all about fertile lying well, hardly any where rocky or with chasms.
a scarcity of black persons

Produce
hay (little or no rye)
wheat little or no flax
oats
barley   *wool* is quite important
potatoes
small-eared corn
   fruits
apples
plums
cherries
all the small fruits in great perfection & plenty
no peaches from the cold
no pears from blight

———

grapes moderate, but they do well

———

Of human stock here in and about in London & perhaps through Ontario, English largely preponderates

———

London is perhaps 50 years old — 40 years ago some twelve or fourteen houses

———

beef
cheese
horses

[NOTES FOR KENNEDY]

Trent Collection catalogue, page 53, number 13. The following fragments are preserved in a scrapbook compiled by William Sloane Kennedy. With the exception of the first two items, they comprise Whitman's comments on a manuscript of a projected book about the poet. Although Kennedy's two books about Whitman were not published until 1896 and 1926, one manuscript was prepared in 1886.[1] *At this time, Whitman read it and returned it with the remarks reproduced here.*

I

Among my special   young men *littérateur* friends are W S Kennedy 7 Waterhouse street Cambridge, Mass: A young college chap — — Greek, Latin, &c — —accepts L of G. —yet bolts at the sexual part — — *but I consider Kennedy as a real & ardent friend both of* self & book[2]

II

Jo Swinton   21 Pk Row,

C. O. B. Bryant.
    Lafayette Hotel

Edwd Howland
     Hammonton   N. Jersey

Wm M. Singerly   Ed Record

H. H. Furness   7th & Locust

Geo H Boker   1720 Walnut

Geo. W. Childs.   2128 Walnut

Horace H Traubel   140 S. 8th

John Swinton.   21 Park Row

[1] *Kennedy*, p. vii.

[2] The following note by Kennedy appears on the manuscript: "Found among the papers of Walt Whitman by Horace Traubel, one of his executors. It is in Whitman's handwriting, & was written in 1881. Given to me by Traubel at the dinner in Boston of the Walt Whitman Fellowship Association on Walt's birthday, May 31, 1896, at Hotel Belleview."

Knortz 540 E 155 st.

Wesley Stafford
Kirkwood
N. J

Geo Stafford,[1]

III

doubtful ab't the "Dedicated to," &c on p 1 —probably *better leave* it out

IV

for *motto* — *Don't like Ruskin's lines* — they are not fitting at all — the other line beginn'g "Allons!" is all right

V

I suggest inquiringly whether it wouldn't be well to put this —adding perhaps what is also marked with red ink on MS page 31 —what I have mark'd on the edge of the sheet with red ink —on the very first page of the text, or introduction — or even on a page by itself at the beginning? —sort of motto

VI

—

pages 26 '7 '8 '9 &c please & satisfy me well[1]

[1] These names and addresses were probably sent to Kennedy for inclusion in the mailing list of the subscription blanks for his proposed book. One such subscription blank is in the Trent Collection.

[1] This fragment bears the following note by Kennedy : "Refers to my book (where I defend the sex poems, imaging an inhabitant of Mars looking over American poetry that has drifted to that planet or been shot there in a projectile &c)." The defense of the sex poems appears in *Kennedy*, pp. 124-125.

VII

page 45 MS

R W Gilder, the now editor of "Century" is a warm admirer of L of G. & personally markedly friendly to W W —The "Century" of Sept. '86 is to contain a short article "Father Taylor (& Oratory)" by W W[1] — Furthermore the "Century" has just taken & handsomely paid for "Army Hospitals & Cases," by W W. & will publish it in due time.[2] see p. 237 your MS.

I have my doubts ab't pages 50 and 51 — I *would leave them out*

VIII

Seems to me this letter of Scovel's is better than Ballou's[1] the one in the Book commenc'g p. 248 — reads better, & gives more desirable information. If you should think so too, substitute it in place of the one Ballou's now in the Book (the MS) — I dont like the latter pages 248 to 255 in Book at all —

[ON STRIKES AND TRAMPS]

Trent Collection catalogue, page 70. Whitman's reaction to the increasing strikes and unemployment which followed the financial crash of 1873 has already been noted and discussed.[1] In the late 1870's the poet planned a lecture on "The Tramp and Strike Questions," and although it was never delivered, he printed some of his notes in Collect.[2] *Additional notes for this lecture have been preserved by Bucke[3] and by Furness.[4] How-*

----

[1] "Father Taylor and Oratory," *Century Magazine*, XXXIII, 583-584 (Feb., 1887).

[2] "Army Hospitals and Cases," *ibid.*, XXXVI, 825-830 (Oct., 1888).

[1] Scovel's comments on Whitman are in *Kennedy*, pp. 11-13, 16-17; and Ballou's interview is in *ibid.*, pp. 13-15.

[1] Newton Arvin, *Whitman* (New York, 1938), pp. 139-144.

[2] *Camden*, V, 284-286.

[3] *Ibid.*, IX, 188-189.　　　　[4] *Furness*, pp. 56-57.

ever, the extent of Whitman's study of the labor problem and his anxiety about its potential dangers were greater than has been previously realized. In the Trent Collection there is a series of forty-eight annotated newspaper and magazine excerpts about this subject. The following notes accompany the clippings.

Excerpts &c Strike & Tramp question
for tramp & strike
I find a large class of our talkers & writers, probably the largest class, always taking for granted that plenty of active manufactures, plenty of money and foreign markets, and a demand by factories, stores, &c. for millions of employes, are the crown'g result and triumph of a nation

Tramps
I shall only be too happy if these black prophecies & fears can be attributed, (as of course they will be,) to my old age and sickness & a growling temper

In America the dangers are, (or shall I say, have been?) from the existence of Slavery Slaves, own'g noth'g, & from the huge collections of ignorant & non-own'g persons, generally immigrants, in the great cities

The communists of France — the radicals &   of
the British Islands — —
the Socialists[5] of Germany —
the   of the—United States
(Tramp & Strike
questions)

[5] Whitman put a question mark above "Socialists."

Letters and Postcards

Trent Collection catalogue, pages 28, 51-58, numbers 39, 2, 4, 5, 9-29, 32-37. These letters and postcards present a typical cross section of Whitman's correspondence between 1861 and 1892. Here are examples which show the poet's fond inclusiveness in his family relationships. The larger number of the letters express his long devotion to his friends, as well as his anxieties over his physical condition and over business transactions. But in all his correspondence Whitman never forgot his primary purpose: the sale and propagation of Leaves of Grass. *During these last thirty years, a period of ill health and limited income, his correspondence was the medium for cultivation of his two major interests: his friendships and his poems. The care with which he nurtured these is evident in the following pages.*

The long series of letters to William Sloane Kennedy provides a detailed picture of the day-to-day life in Camden. The story of Whitman's friendship with Kennedy is well known, and excerpts from some of these letters have already been published.[1]

The other letters in this section, with their accompanying identifications, yield further information about Whitman's life. In order to preserve the chronology, the correspondence is arranged by date instead of by recipient.

To George Whitman

[B]rooklyn,
July 12th, 1861.

Dear Brother,[1]

Your letter come to-day. Every thing with us is pretty

---

[1] See *Kennedy*, pp. 49-68. Letters from Whitman to Kennedy have been edited also by Oral S. Coad ("Seven Whitman Letters," *Journal of the Rutgers University Library*, VIII, 18-26, Dec., 1944).

[1] At the time this letter was written, George W. Whitman was serving his

much the same. Mother is pretty much the same. Some days she [is] better, and some not so well. She has taken a good many sulphur vapor baths. She takes one every other day. She goes down in the cars to the baths, in Willoughby street near the City Hall. Sometimes Mat goes with her, a while she goes [alo]ne. They are rather agreeable to take —they make one sweat extremely. Mother goes about the same, around the house. She has better use of her arms and wrists than she did there one time — but an hour or two, now and then, generally in the morning, she has bad pains. Her appetite is pretty good. — The weather here lately has been awful — three days the heat was as bad as I ever knew it —so I think that had something to do with mother's feeling weak. To-day it is much cooler.

Jeff and Martha and Cis and Eddy are all well. Jess is the same as usual — he works every day in the yard. He does not seem to mind the heat. He is employed in the store-house, where they are continually busy preparing stores, provisions, to send off in the different vessels. He assists in that.

We are all very glad the 13th is coming home — mother especially. There have been so many accounts of shameful negligence, or worse, in the commissariat of your reg't. that there must be *something* in it — notwithstand'g you speak very lightly of the complaints in your letters. The *Eagle* of course, makes the worst of it, every day, to stop men from enlisting.

All of us here think the rebellion as good as broke — no matter if the war does continue for months yet.

Walt.

---

term of one hundred days with the Brooklyn Thirteenth Regiment, prior to regular enlistment.

To Dr. Le Baron Russell [?]

[February, 1864][1]

The hospitals here in & around Washington are still pretty full, and contain in some respects the most needy cases of all the suffer'g — (though there are plenty such every where.) For the past few weeks I have been on a tour down to the front, through the division hospitals especially those around Culpepper & Brandy Station, mostly of the 1st, 2d, & 3d corps to see how the sick were situated there. A year ago I spent December & part of January (after 1st Fredericksburgh) among the wounded in front from Aquia Creek to Falmouth, and saw perhaps the saddest scenes of the war then. But there is noth'g like it now. I have made up my mind that—the camp hospitals are pretty well cleaned out, the worst cases are here in Washington, & so I have returned here for good. In the field hospitals I find diarrhea, gett'g more & more prevalent, & chronic. It is the great disease of the army. The doctors, as always, give too much medicine, & hold on to the poor young men in camp too long, then when the the   is deeply rooted, send them up here. how many such wrecks of young men have I seen, from boat & railroad, from front, come crawl'g pale & faint along here, many to linger a while & die, dur'g the past year, sent up, in this way after be'g kept too long.[2]

I suppose you will be interested in know'g that our troops in the field in Virginia are this Winter remarkably

[1] A slip of paper accompanying this manuscript bears the following inscription: "February 1864 Down in the Army at Culpepper & Brandy Station — describe field hospitals, &c." Dr. Le Baron Russell, of Boston, collected and contributed money which was forwarded to Whitman for distribution among the sick and wounded (*Donaldson*, pp. 145-152; *Glicksberg*, p. 100). Excerpts from this draft of a letter were also used in the New York *Times* for Dec. 11, 1864, and reprinted as "Hospital Visits" in *The Wound Dresser* (Boston, 1898), pp. 21-46.

[2] For another version of this paragraph, see *The Wound Dresser*, pp. 33-34.

well in health, however, as a general thing & in the cheeri-
est temper. They have better houses than ever before, no
shelter tents now, but huts of logs & mud, with fireplaces In
the tour I allude to, I was much in contact with the rank in
file, lived amg them in their camps, amg the common soldiers
& teamsters, &c. I never go amg the Army in this way, but
what, after mak'g all allowances, I feel that our general
stock of young men shows all other races, meagre & pale &
puny in comparison. The more I see of them in the army,
the higher & broader my estimate of them. (I mean
the Americans, I dont make account of any other —
Americans both west & East, & from all the agricultural
regions of the great states) And then to be amg them also as
I have been for past fifteen months, amg them, see'g them
in hospitals thousands, so young & manly, with such fearful
suffering, wounds, amputations, & weary sickness. O how one
gets to love them, — indeed it brings people very, very
close, such circumstances.

As to the temper of the Army in Virginia I should say
it was never so resolute, so full of the right spirit for endur-
ance & work as it is to-day. The filled-up regiments,
gather'g around the nucleus of the old veterans, make better
regiments than any. I was with several such, & found them
excellent. These re-enlisted regiments, return'g from their
furloughs, thus filled up, are stream'g down to front fast
already. The opinion of Meade is full of respect for him,
— he is thought an earnest, alert, conscientious, cautious com-
mander.

I write these, doctor, think'g they may interest you,
com'g from late direct contact with the army on the ground.

So doctor I still remain here in Washington, occupy'g
my time nearly altogether among the wounded & sick as when
I last wrote you.[3] I act as an independent visitor & helper

[3] Whitman wrote to Dr. Russell on December–3, 1863 (*Glicksberg*, p.
140).

among the men, fix'g as before on the cases that most need.
I I never miss a single day or night, week day or Sunday
visit'g some poor, young soul in bodily & mental tribulation.
It is a great privilege to me, more to me than to them I
think

To an Editor

[December, 1864]

Sir: whether it agrees with your own opinion or not I
hope you will open your columns to this communication of
mine,[1] seek'g to stir up the governmnt to a general exchange
of prisoners. I hope also you may feel to say a word about it
editorially,—if you could call attention to it.

As I have sent similar communications this afternoon to
one or two other papers, I would particularly solicit that
you find room for it in to-morrow's issue.

To Dion Thomas

Dion Thomas[1]
Nassau st. bet Beekman & Spru

Washington   Oct. 13 [1867]

Dear Sir:

I write to ask your kind offices in the following described
matter:

I sent to Doolady[2] six weeks ago an order

Mr. James Gray, Bookbinder 16 Spruce st. 4th floor, is
the custodian of the sheets of my Leaves of Grass, & has
been the binder for me. The sheets are now at his place.

I hear that he has become involved — in fact has failed.[3]

---

[1] The present manuscript is a draft of a letter enclosing a communication
which was printed in the Brooklyn *Daily Eagle* and in the New York *Times*
for Dec. 27, 1864 (reprinted in *Glicksberg*, pp. 178-180).

[1] Thomas was the owner of a bookshop at 142 Nassau Street. The present
manuscript is a canceled draft.

[2] Michael Doolady was the owner of a bookshop at 448 Broome Street.

[3] There is no record of the bankruptcy, but, according to Whitman, "the
place had been seized for debt" (*Traubel*, II, 257).

If so, I regret it much.

I have been wait'g now over six weeks for the fulfilment of orders I have sent him for bound books — & now, under that state of things, I suppose it will not be possible for him to do the work.

To William D. O'Connor

Oct 4 [1868] ask about the office — Ashton[1] —has Andy Kerr[2] returned — my new desk

Dear friend,

I suppose you rec'd my letter of 25th September. The letters sent by you from A. G. office, (I suppose sent by you) have probably all come right. I have received some five or six. Please continue to send them in same way. If the envelopes run out please prepare some more same address. If you write, tell me what news in the A. G. office. Is Ashton runn'g the office? Is he well? Say to him I sent my love — & that it seems to me, by appearances hereabout even, the Grant & Colfax tide is rising higher & higher every day.

Tell Charles Eldridge

Did you see John Swintons warm ¶ about my illustrious self in N. Y. Times, 1st inst.?[3]—John seems lately possest with L. of G. as with a demon. I have found two or three others —a Mr. Norton, of Boston— is one. He is an educated man, a Boston metaphysical thinker. — Give my best love to John Burroughs, & lend him this note to read. J. B., dear friend, I wish I could have you here, if only just to take a ride with me for once up & down Broadway, on top of a stage in the height of the jam & etc

[1] J. Hubley Ashton, Assistant Attorney-General (1864-1867, 1868-1869). The present manuscript is the draft of a letter now in the Berg Collection, New York Public Library.

[2] Andrew L. Kerr was a clerk in the office of the Attorney-General from May 27, 1861, to Sept. 1, 1869 (letter from Gerald J. Davis, National Archives, Feb. 11, 1946).

[3] New York *Times* for Oct. 1, 1868.

To John Burroughs

Providence, R. I.
October 22, 1868.

Dear friend,

I have been thinking about you this morning, and will write a few lines, though without any thing special to communicate. My vacation is nearly done, & in four or five days more I shall be back in Washington. I have been here in Providence the past week, as guest of Thomas Davis, a manufacturer here, & formerly M.C.[1] — have had a good time generally, in a quiet way — am going on to New York this afternoon, & shall be back in Washington on the 27th — William O'Connor is here in Providence — I have been with him a good deal — he is not very well, but goes around. — Will finish my letter in New York, & mail it thence tomorrow.

Walt.

To John Townsend Trowbridge

107 north Portland av.
Brooklyn, N. Y.
Sept. 24. [1870]

My dear friend,

I am here a while on leave — am in good health as usual —have been engaged in electrotyping a new edition of my book &c in better form — You sent me word a year or more ago of some Boston publisher, or bookseller, who was willing, (or perhaps wished) to sell my book[1] — Who

---

[1] Thomas Davis, Member of Congress (1853-1855), was a partner of Sackett, Davis & Co., manufacturing jewelers, Providence, R. I. (letter from Henry G. Jackson, May 31, 1945). The present letter is mentioned, but not printed, in *Barrus*, p. 57.

[1] The letter referred to is printed in *Traubel*, III, 506-507. Cf. the statement: "Mr. Trowbridge tells me he discovered a seller of antique books in Boston who consented to put his imprint on a small edition of Leaves of Grass. But Walt Whitman wrote me that he knew of no such edition" (*Kennedy*, p. 17 n.). Whitman's letter to Kennedy is printed on pp. 104-105.

was it? — I should like to have some such man there — to sell the book on commission, & be agent, depositor, &c — He will be under no expense, of course & will only receive the books from me on sale — I wish to put his name in an advertisement list of agents —

Please answer forthwith —direct to me here.

Yours as ever
Walt Whitman

no objection to a couple of such Boston booksellg places—as agencies
Love to the son, —dear boy.[2]

To JAMES C. MCGUIRE

Washington,
May 2, 1872.

My dear Mr. McGuire,[1]

The money you gave me for Mr. Tasistro[2] has been handed by me to him, and has substantially helped him. I have been out to see him several times since I met you — he is up & about & in much better spirits — has great thoughts of getting well, & going to work to earn his living himself.

He has had a very hard time dur'g the winter — Can never again be strong & well — but has indomitable vitality.

Walt Whitman

[2] Windsor Warren Trowbridge (1864-1884).

[1] James C. McGuire (1812-1888), of Washington, D. C., a collector of Americana.

[2] Count Michael Tasistro, teacher and translator, is frequently mentioned by Whitman in the letters to Pete Doyle (*Calamus*, pp. 95, 103, 108, 110, 154, 161).

To James M. Edmunds

Nov. 17 [1872?]

J M Edmunds, P. M.[1]

Dear Sir:

Your letter, referr'g me the ruling of the P. O. Dept. is to what the term *"book manuscripts"* as usued in Sec. 244. Postal Laws. and Reg. includes, and what it excludes, makes me then respectfully request that if convenient, that ruling shall be brought up before the proper officers, of the Dept to be reconsidered and reversed for the follow'g briefly stated reasons:

1st the word "Book" as used in the statute is unquestionably the generic term "Book," comprehensive of all printed literary matter, (see Webster's Unabridged Dict. last ed. p. 151.) A pamphlet, monthly or weekly magazine, the "Living Age" the "Galaxy," or any literary composition, or printed issue, or any collection of sheets of paper, of literary character, or only two sheets, or one sheet, — must, all & several, be included in the term.

2d. The intention of Congress by very much of of its post office, & other legislation to foster literature, education, authorship, general reead'g, publication, &c. & be liberal to the press: is well known to the Dept. I might claim therefore that The section must be construed generously. But I merely claim that it be construed accord'g to the exact mean'g & definition of its own terminology

— See the Dictionaries

Webster — Book—a general name of of every printed literary composition

$\overline{\bullet}$ . . . .

The quest. a generic term   The question also is, Is a magazine — (i. e. a pamphlet) — a book — See dictionary

---

[1] James M. Edmunds, Postmaster, Washington, D. C. (1869-1880). The present manuscript is a preliminary draft.

—*pamphlet*........a small book
Worcester—*pamphlet* — ....
.... a book consisting of only
one or a few sheets stitched together, & not
bound —

I would respectfully apply a second time for a reconsideration & reversal of the ruling of the construction in your Dept. of that proviso of Sec. 244 of Postal Laws, which fixes the postage on "book Manuscripts and corrected proofs passing between authors & publishers," at the rate of ordinary printed matter which ruling, as furnished me, is that MSS. and corrected proofs from or to *Magazines, pamphlets,* literary *periodicals,* &c. are *not* included in this proviso, but shall pay letter postage.

Against this I again offer as follows:

The main question is, What is a book in fact, and in the mean'g of the law? — I say, in both, it is

In the ruling furnished me by the Department, stress is laid on the *distinction* Congress makes (in the postage rate) between *Books* and and other printed matter, as pamphlets, magazines, & newspapers. So they do make such distinction, *invariably in order to decrease the rate of postage of* the *latter.* ¶ The inference is a fair one then that if book MSS go for printed matter postage, the pamphlet and magazine MSS should at least do so.)—

The distinction is made for the purpose of to *favoring* the periodical press. But It does not warrant any such inference as in the rul'g furnished.

All *literary* MSS. are "book manuscripts," and when printed, they become "Books" — and the law covers *all* (literary matter) — To contend otherwise would be same as to confine the meaning of the word *man* as used by metaphysicians and statesmen by Jefferson in the Declaration of Independence for instance,) to mean the full grown a full grown *male person only* — while, of course, it is an ensemble and generic term, for both sexes, and all ages.

To Louisa Van Velsor Whitman

[Before May 23, 1873]
Write how George & Smith make out — George, how would it do for you to put up a couple of small houses to be worth about $2000 a piece, in some good spot, outer part of the city — one of the two for *us* — & the other for sale — I could raise $800 cash — to leave 1200 on bond & mortgage — some such plan — You & Smith could do much of the work yourselves — I only mention it to see whether it would be practicable. Good bye dear mother

Walt.

[On verso:]
not sick with rheumatism or any thing — I see the carpenters in Brooklyn are demanding $4 a day — I was think'g perhaps George & Smith would just take

To Louisa Van Velsor Whitman

[Before May 23, 1873]
Mother I will write only a short letter this time, as I have a good deal of work to do to-day in the office. —
— Every thing goes on with me just the same as usual
— I hope you are feeling well, dear mother, & the rest too.

Walt

To Charles W. Eldridge

322 Stevens st. Camden, N. J.
Monday afternoon June 23d [1873]
Dear Charley,
I have now been a week here, & am about the same — well enough to keep up and around, but with bad spells

most every day, & sometimes very bad ones. My head does not get right, that being still the trouble — the feeling now being as if it were in the centre of the head, heavy & painful & quite pervading — locomotion about the same — no better.[1] I keep pretty good spirits, however, & still make my calculations on getting well. I am pleasantly situated here — have two nice rooms, second floor, with windows north & south, if there is any air. They are the rooms in which my mother died, with all the accustomed furniture, I have long been so used to see. I am quite satisfied here, so far — Sleep good, & appetite sufficient. It has been warm weather here, but I have stood it fairly. I hear by your letter & the papers it has been very oppressively hot in Washington. To-day, as I write, it is cloudy & cooler here. I have not felt well enough yet to strike out for Atlantic City.

Charley I rec'd your letter Saturday, with the one enclosed. (It was a very kind sympathetic note from Kate Hillard.) I have written to Harry Douglas, my fellow clerk in the office, asking him to send me my letters here under frank from the office, till July 1st — I am glad to hear Nelly[2] is feeling better — I hope quite well — I send my best love to her — please hand her this letter to read — Nelly I still feel that I shall pull through, but O it is a weary, weary pull, — & when I have these spells in the head that still afflict me, it requires all my phlegm

My lift at the Ashton's was a great help to me[3] — the

---

[1] This letter was written after the death of Whitman's mother on May 23, 1873. On June 15 Whitman began a two months' leave of absence, but he never returned to his position as clerk in the Department of Justice (Dixon Wecter, "Walt Whitman as Civil Servant," *PMLA*, LVIII, 1106, Dec., 1943).

[2] Ellen M. (Mrs. William D.) O'Connor.

[3] In a letter to John Burroughs, dated June 26, 1873, Eldridge wrote that Whitman "was not content to stay at his room so he availed himself of the invitation of the Ashtons and went up there and staid for ten or twelve days" (*Barrus*, p. 83).

change from the 15th st. rooms, & then the weather being so favorable — the change here is so far good, too — As soon as I get a little stronger, & free from head-distress, I shall go down to Atlantic city —

— Remember me to Dr. Drinkard[4] if you see him, & if you have a good chance read to him what I have said of my case — if he has any suggestions, write me —

Charley I have amused myself with *Kenelm Chillingly* — read it all — like it well — Bulwer is *such a snob* as almost redeems snobdom — — the story is good, & the style a master's — Like Cervantes, Bulwer's old-age-productions are incomparably his best. Lend me a Chronicle occasionally.

Walt.

To Charles W. Eldridge

322 Stevens st.
Camden, N. J.
Monday forenoon July 7. [1873]

Dear Charley,

Your letter came last week, enclosing one from the office. I have just written to the Postmaster at Washington, asking him to forward my letters here, as I suppose that can be done. How is it? Can it be done — do you know? So you are to leave Washington on Thursday next — & Nelly and Jeannie[1] are also — for a New England visit —May it be a pleasant & healthful & happy one for all of you.

In my case there is no notable amendment — — & not much change — I have irregular spells of serious distress, pain &c. in the head, full as bad as ever, sometimes lasting all day, & sometimes part of the day or night only, with in-

---

[4] William B. Drinkard (1842-1877) was Whitman's Washington physician.

[1] The daughter of Mr. and Mrs. William D. O'Connor.

tervals in which, (while I remain still,) I feel comparatively
easy — but my locomotion is about as bad as it was — last
evening I thought it worse than usual — (to-day it is not)
— I am not taking any medicine, nor have I talked with any
doctor since I left W. — Nights & sleep are quite good —
appetite middl'g — &c &c. — I still stay here, afraid to go
to Atlantic City, or any where, while I am liable every day
to these depressing spells — & incapacitated from walking —
— We have the weather in *streaks* of hot & cool here — last
evening it turned coldish, & remains so this forenoon, very
bright & pleasant —but we had it very hot here too, some
days — by what I see in the *Phil. Ledger* and N. Y. Herald
Wash. items to-day,[2] I infer that William has rec'd the ap-
pointment of C. C. at which I am *truly pleased* —

—Nelly, as I suppose you will see this letter, I will send
you my love, in it, and you must take this letter the same
as if written to you — I wont ask you to write from W. at
present in the midst of your preparations — but write me
from Newport, after you get well rested & settled — did
you see Dr. Drinkard? & did he say any thing new about my
sickness or symptoms?—

— I have rec'd a letter from John Burroughs to-day —
he & wife are evidently having real good healthy country
times away there in the cool uplands of Delaware county —
he is home —

I am feeling comparatively comfortable to-day, & still
hope for the best — *but* —

— Charley go in to my office a moment, before you go, &
see if any letters — tell me if William is definitely appointed — write very soon from Boston, if not before. Walt.

[2] "Lighthouse Officer," New York *Herald* for July 7, 1873; "Personal,"
Public Ledger for July 7, 1873. "William" is W. D. O'Connor.

To Henry M. Alden

431 Stevens st.
cor West

Camden, N. Jersey.
Nov. 2, 1873.

Editor Harpers' Magazine,[1]
Dear Sir,

I offer the "*Song of the Redwood Tree*," herewith, for your consideration for the Magazine.[2] The price is $100. If accepted send me a proof here when put in type. If not available would you do me the favor to return the MS. by mail without delay.

Walt Whitman.

I reserve the right to print the piece in future book.

To Trübner & Company

431 Stevens st.
Camden, New Jersey.
U. S. America.

Messrs. Trübner & Company,
Dear Sirs,

Please make out acc't of sales of my books, *Leaves of Grass* &c. for the closing year, & remit me am't due, by mail here, by draft payable to my order.

Respectfully &c.
Walt Whitman

Dec. 27,
1873.

[1] Henry M. Alden, editor (1869-1919) of *Harper's New Monthly Magazine.*
[2] "Song of the Redwood-Tree," *Harper's New Monthly Magazine,* XLVIII, 366-367 (Feb., 1874).

To William Stansberry

May 20, '74

Dear Wm. Stansberry,[1]

I will just write you a few lines off-hand. Your letter of May 14 has come to hand, to-day reminding me of your being in Armory Square Hospital & of my visits there, & meeting you, in '65. Your writing, or someth'g it has started, strangely, deeply touches me. It takes me back to the scenes of ten years ago, in the war, the hospitals of Washington, the many wounded bro't up after the battles, and the never-to-be told sights of suffering & death. To think that the little gift & word of kindness, should be remembered by you so long — & that the kiss I gave you amid those scenes, should be treasured up, & as it were sent back to me after many years! Dear Comrade — you do me good, by your loving wishes & feelings to me in your letter. (I send you my love, & to your dear children & wife the same. As I write, you seem very dear to me too, like some young brother, who has been lost, but now found.

—whether we shall ever meet each other is doubtful — probably we never will — but I feel that we should both be happy, if we could be together — (I find there are some that it is just comfort enough to be together, almost without any th'g else) —

I remain about the same in my sickness. I sleep & eat pretty well — go about some, look stout & red, (though looking now *very* old & gray, but that is noth'g new,) — weigh 185 now — am badly lamed in my left leg, & have bad spells, of occasional days, feebleness distress in head, &c. I think I shall get well yet, but may not. Have been

[1] The records of the Adjutant General's office show that William Stansberry (b. 1837) served in the Third West Virginia Cavalry from March 16, 1865, to July 27, 1865. He was one of "the typical soldiers I have been personally intimate with" (*Camden*, IV, 134). This draft was prepared in answer to a letter, dated May 12, 1874, which is in the Trent Collection.

laid up here a year dog noth'g, except a little writ'g. As far as room, food, care, &c. are concerned, I am well situated here — but *very lonesome* — have no near friends, (in the deepest sense) here at hand — — my mother died here a year ago — a sorrow from which I have never entirely recovered, & likely never shall — she was an unusually noble, cheerful woman — very proud-spirited & generous — am poor, (yet with a little income, & means, just enough to pay my way, with strict economy, to be independent of want)

TO MR. AND MRS. JOHN BURROUGHS

431 Stevens st.
cor West.

Camden
N. Jersey.
March 2. [1875]

Dear John, & 'Sula,

This will show you 'that "the lamp still holds out to burn" — though I have had a bad two months past — I have had another paralytic stroke, but it passed over, without any thing serious, (it is probable I have had several slight strokes) — but I am feeling, as I write, about the same as is now usual for me — still entertain expectations — — If practicable I shall bring out a Vol. the com'g summer — I hope to pay you *the visit* yet

— Did you get the paper I sent with a report of Emerson's late lecture on *Eloquence* — of course interesting, from him, but nothing very stunning, it seemed to me. — I see that Conway is coming to America next autumn certain, to see things, travel, lecture, &c

— John I send you the the last letter from a quondam correspondent & unseen rebel friend of mine, away down in Alabama[1] — He seems to me a good affectionate fellow, a

[1] John Newton Johnson, whose letters are described in *Barrus*, pp. 92-93.

sort of uncut gem —I have had five or six letters from him
all primitive but good What are *you* about? — & how are
you & 'Sula getting along?

Walt Whitman

My brother & sister well
  — brother full of business

To Edward Dowden

431 Stevens st.
cor. West.

Camden,
N. Jersey.
U. S. America.
March 4,/76

Dear friend,

Yours of Feb. 6[1] with draft reach'd me which I re-
sponded to, sending new edition ["Le]aves of Grass" and
"Two Rivulets," two or three days since, by mail, same address as this, which you ought to have rec'd now lately —
sent postal card briefly notifying you, & asking you to send
me word (by postal card will do) immediately on their reception.

To-day comes your affectionate, hearty, valued letter of
Feb. 16,[2] all right, with enclosure draft 12L. 10s-, —all
deeply appreciated — the *letter* good, cannot be better, but,
as always, the *spirit* the main thing — (altogether like some
fresh, magnetic, friendly breath of breeze, 'way off there
from the Irish Coast) —I wonder if you can know how much
good such things do me. I shall send the six sets, (six
"Leaves" and six "Rivulets") by express, very soon, (probably by next Philadelphia steamer.) The extra copies of
"Memoranda of the War" not being ready bound, at present,
I will send by mail — six copies, before very long. (I
hope the set above mention'd I mailed you by last steamer,

---

[1] Dowden's letter is printed in *Traubel*, I, 299-301.
[2] The letter is printed in *ibid.*, I, 301-303.

will have reach'd you before you get this.) I saw O'Grady's article in the December "Gentleman's"[3] & from my point of view, he dwells on *what I like to have dwelt on.* I was deeply pleased with the article, & if I had O'Grady's address I would like to send him my photograph. I also read the Peter Bayne article.[4] (It was copied in full here at once, & circulated quite largely.) As I write this, I have not read Abraham Stoker's letter, but shall do so, & carefully. (The names shall be written in the Vols. as you mention.) I read with great zest the account of the discussion at the "Fortnightly" — I have learn'd to feel *very thankful* to those who attack & abuse & pervert me — that's perhaps (besides being good fun) the only way to bring out the splendid ardor & friendship of those, my unknown friends, my best reward, art & part with me, in my pages, (for I have come to solace & perhaps flatter myself that it is *they* indeed in them, as much as *I*, every bit.)

My condition physically is pretty much the same — no worse, at least not decidedly. I get out nearly every day, but not far, & cannot walk from lameness — — make much of the river here, the broad Delaware, cross'g a great deal on the ferry, full of life & fun to me — get down there by our horse cars, which run along near my door — — get infinite kindness, care, & assistance, from the employés on these boats & cars — My friend, next time you write, say more about yourself, family & Mrs. Dowden, to whom with yourself best love & regards — Walt Whitman

[3] Arthur Clive [Standish O'Grady], "Walt Whitman, the Poet of Joy," *Gentleman's Magazine*, N.S., XV, 704-716 (Dec., 1875).

[4] Peter Bayne, "Walt Whitman's Poems," *Contemporary Review*, XXVII, 49-69 (December, 1875). This article was reprinted in the *Living Age*, CXXVIII, 91-103 (Jan. 8, 1876).

POSTCARD TO EDWARD CARPENTER

Camden   New Jersey
U S America

Oct 5 [1877]—I have to-day sent by mail post paid, the Volumes to Messrs *Thompson, Templeton, Teall* and *Haweis*,[1] (seven Vols in all) — *Many thanks to you* —I am well, for me — I am just going over to the G's[2] to spend the evening — H[3] has return'd —

W W

POSTCARD TO EDWARD CARPENTER

Camden New Jersey,
U S America

Nov 27 [1877] — Your card of Nov 13 rec'd — I have to-day mailed Mr Vines' books[1] — —Your card of a week or ten days previous rec'd — Many & sincere thanks — — I still keep pretty well, & every thing goes on with me much as usual —

—Geo: Stafford has been very ill with hemorrhages from the stomach (hematemesis) but is over it, & out, though feeble — the rest well — — the Gilchrists are all well —Mrs G is here with us in Camden today to dinner —we often speak of you — WW

[1] On Dec. 19, 1877, Carpenter sent a letter to Whitman stating: "I hear from Vines that your books have arrived. He and Thompson (to whom you sent before) are lecturers at Cambridge, Haweis is a popular London preacher, Templeton is working music in London—organizing cheap concerts &c. — and Teall is teaching science at Nottingham. . . . So you see the kind of audience you have" (*Traubel*, I, 189).

[2] At this time Mrs. Anne Gilchrist lived at 1929 North Twenty-second street, Philadelphia (*The Letters of Anne Gilchrist and Walt Whitman*, ed. Thomas B. Harned, Garden City, 1918, p. xxxiii).

[3] Herbert Harlakenden Gilchrist, son of Anne Gilchrist.

[1] See preceding postcard, n.1.

To A. Williams & Co.

431 Stevens Street
Camden New Jersey
Nov 30 '77

A. Williams & Co[1]
Dear Sirs

In compliance with your request of Nov 28 I send by Adams's Express three copies of the only edition of *Leaves of Grass,* of the few copies at my command to fulfil your order — (the retail price is $3) —below see bill, the am't which please remit me here.

Walt Whitman

Bill   Camden N J Nov
                                                 30 '77

A. Williams & Co
To W Whitman
To three Copies Leaves
          of Grass @ $1.75   —$5.25
      Rec'd Payment

Postcard to John Burroughs

1309 Fifth av.   2d house south of 86th st.[1]
New York July 5 [1878] — Still here —still quite well
— — sent you a paper yesterday with my "June" letter in[2]
— — Shall go back to Camden ab't the 10th (or 9th) —
Fiery weather here, but I stand it well so far   WW

[1] A. Williams & Co. owned the "Old Corner Bookstore" in Boston from 1864 to 1883.

[1] Home of Mr. and Mrs. J. H. Johnston.
[2] "A Poet's Recreation," New York *Daily Tribune* for July 4, 1878.

To Trübner & Co. [?]

431 Stevens Street
Camden New Jersey U S America
Oct 1 '78 —

Dear Sirs

Yours of Sept 14 with $14 for Two Sets (4 Vols) of my books has come safely to hand — thank you sincerely — — I to-day forward to Wiley & Sons, New York, Twelve Sets (24 Vols) of my books, to be sent you — which please acknowledge as soon as received — Two of the Twelve Sets being paid for, there are Ten Sets, for which you are to acc't to me at $7 the set — & you are not to furnish them to purchasers at less than $10 the set, or $5 the Vol.

Walt Whitman

To George Waters

Camden   New Jersey
Nov 10 '78

Dear George Waters[1]

Yours of 4th rec'd (I only came up yesterday from the country, where I go more than half the time) — I am pretty well for me, & have had a good summer — Will the enclosed little bit do for your publication?[2] — Success to it —

Walt Whitman

George if you print it be very careful of the proof — they have lately made some bad work in that respect for me —

[1] George Waters (1832-1912), of Elmira, N. Y., artist.
[2] We have no record of the "publication."

To Samuel Van Wyck

1309 Fifth av: near 86th street.

May 28 '79

My dear Sir[1]

Yours of May 23d has reach'd me here —I am unable to give you any information on the genealogic points you speak of —wish I could — — I have an idea there are town records or documents at Huntington, that are accessible, & that might throw light on the Van Wyck and Whitman families — I have seen such records alluded to, & printed extracts from them — where they are, or what office, *in Huntington* I think or who keeps them, I can not say — Yes, I was born at West Hills — my father Walter Whitman I trace the Whitmans there four generations —my grandmother (fathers mother) was Hannah *Brush* —— I am here on a visit —— go back, last of next week, to Camden New Jersey, my regular p o address.

Walt Whitman

Postcard to T. W. H. Rolleston

431 Stevens Street

Camden   New Jersey   U S America

Dec: 2 [1880] — Ev'ng —Rec'd to-day a copy of your *Encheiridion*[1] — seems a little beauty of book making.   I suppose you have rec'd the copies of new L of G. I sent you over three weeks since, addressed same as this card.

Walt Whitman

[1] Samuel Van Wyck (1824-1910), of Brooklyn, N. Y., merchant.

[1] Rolleston's letter presenting a copy of his edition of Epictetus, Oct. 16, 1880, is printed in *Traubel*, II, 67-69. Whitman's affection for the book is expressed in an inscription on an end-paper: "from 1881 to '88 — Have had this little Vol. at hand or in my hand often, all these years —" (*ibid.*, III, 253).

To Thomas Nicholson

431 Stevens street
Camden New Jersey U S A — Dec: 17 [1880]
Dear Tom[1]

I was glad to have word from you once more, & glad to get the particulars of that race — this is the first full account I have heard, & I am real pleased Tommy first at the satisfaction of your winning, and next at your raking in the good stakes — altogether it must have been quite a time

Yes Dr Bucke was here, and we had a very pleasant afternoon and evening together — had a first rate dinner —and then in the hotel sitting room some of the tallest kind of talking & arguing you may be sure.

I live very quietly & plainly here, board with my brother & sister in law — have a nice little room up in the third story fronting south, (I am sitting here now in a great rocking chair, & the sun is pouring in bright and warm as you please — I wish you was here Tommy to spend the afternoon with me) — — I have some work to day, most every day a little, but I take it easy, content if I can make enough to pay my expenses —I never cared to be rich, (no possibility of that any how) but I dont care to be too poor either.

I get out on the river, (the Delaware) or over in Philadelphia most every day — lately I go down to the Ferry at nights & cross over & back two or three times. The river is full of ice & the boats have a pretty tough time —but the nights are light, the full moon, shining like silver and I enjoy it all — (know the pilots and boat hands intimately.) Last night was perfect, & only middl'g cool — I staid crossing till 12 o'clock, — felt good, —& then got hungry & went and got a dozen nice oysters & a drink (Dont that make your mouth water Tommy boy?) I often think of you and

[1] Thomas Nicholson was an attendant at the Asylum in London, Ontario (letter from M. Alice Martin, Jan. 9, 1946).

the boys & girls — give my best respects to all of them Dick
Flynn, Tom Bradley[2] & all the cricket boys — that was the
best summer there in Canada, & among you all & the Asylum
grounds, & the daily rides into London & all, that I ever put
in & I am feeling the benefit of it yet. My love to you Tom
& am glad you dont forget me, as I won't you —try to write
to me regular —

Walt Whitman

Did George England's[3] picture come all safe?

Postcard to William Sloane Kennedy

Camden N J   Feb: 25 [1881]
Evening

Thanks — If convenient then send me the Carlyle
Tribune[1] — & I will return.

Walt Whitman

To Thomas Nicholson

Camden New Jersey U S America
March 17 '81

Dear Tom

Your letter has just come all right & I am glad to
hear from you again. Every thing seems to go lovely there
with you & the boys & Dr B (which is as it should be)
—Tom I often think of you all, & of the last night we all
got together, & of the friendly parting drink we all had out
there on the lawn — seems as if I only got to know you & all

---

[2] Flynn and Bradley were also employed at the Asylum. Bradley was
"the man who drove Dr. Bucke and Walt Whitman to the city of London
and back to the Asylum during the time of Walt Whitman's stay" (letter
from Edwin Seaborn, Nov. 15, 1944).

[3] "The Englands lived at the side gate and had as part of their duties the
closing of this gate in the evening" (letter from Edwin Seaborn, Dec. 8,
1945).

[1] Nine excerpts from articles about Thomas Carlyle in the New York *Daily
Tribune* for Feb. 21, 1881.

best & then time for me to clear out — — I have some good times here in moderation — I cant go around very lively, but I enjoy what's going on wherever I go — This 31st of May coming I shall be 62 — but thank the Lord I still feel young at heart & cheery as ever —After I returned last fall from Canada I was first rate all along — put in four good months — had some rare old times —will tell you when we meet, Tom — but some six weeks ago was careless enough to get badly chill'd all through my whole body, & repeated the next day — so I have been since quite under the weather — But I am getting over it, & feeling quite myself again — — I find I can be well enough if I take very particular care of myself, how I go, &c An old doctor here said to me "Whitman you are like an old wagon, built of first rate stuff, & the best sort of frame & wheels & nuts —& as long as you are mighty careful, & go slow, & *keep to good roads*, you will last as long as any of us —but if you get on bad roads, or cut up any capers, then *look out*" — I go down every week or two (I go tomorrow again) about 20 miles from here right into the country, with a family of farmers, dear friends of mine, named Stafford — keep a country store also — a big family of boys & girls, & Mrs S one of the kindest & best women in the world how much happier one can be when there is good women around — Does me good to be with them all. Every thing is very old fashioned, just suits me —good grub & plenty of it. My great loafing place out there is a big old woods, mostly pine & oak, but lots of laurel & holly, old paths & roads every where through the thick woods —I spend hours there every day —have it all to myself —go out there well-protected, even in a snow storm — rabbits & squirrels, & lots of birds beginn'g already —Tom you would laugh to see me the way I amuse myself, often spouting terrible pieces from

Shakspere or Homer as loud as I can yell. (But that always was a favorite practice of mine — I used to do it in the din of Broadway New York from the top of an omnibus —at other times along the seashore at Coney Island) — — Tom my paper is fill'd & I must close — I wanted to write something about the running & matches, but must postpone it — Give my love to all my friends there & you keep a good big share for yourself dear boy —

Walt Whitman

To William Sloane Kennedy

431 Stevens Street
Camden New Jersey Dec 21 '81

My dear W S K

Yours rec'd & glad to hear from you — have not forgotten those pleasant calls & chats, & hope they will one day be renewed — I read your (added to & somewhat changed) California magazine criticism[1] — the copy you showed Osgood — & thought it noble — — Am thankful to you & of course much pleased with your study of, & exploiting L of G —have just sent you a package by express of the late & other editions & Vols. of poems &c. as my Christmas offering — with affectionate remembrances

Walt Whitman[2]

Postcard to William Sloane Kennedy

Camden New Jersey
May 24 '82

Thanks for the beautiful & opportune book[1] — just come to hand — — I am about as usual in health —

Walt Whitman

[1] William Sloane Kennedy, "A Study of Walt Whitman," *Californian*, III, 149-158 (Feb., 1881).

[2] The following note appears at the end of the letter: "I afterward sent him $5. as part payment for these K."

[1] The book is probably William Sloane Kennedy, *Henry W. Longfellow* (Cambridge, Mass., 1882).

POSTCARD TO WILLIAM SLOANE KENNEDY

431 Stevens Street
Camden   New Jersey   Nov: 28 '82

I have just returned from a two week's visit down in the Jersey woods where I go occasionally — & find your most interesting "Whittier"[1]— Thank you heartily.   I am again about as usual in health—   Walt Whitman

POSTCARD TO WILLIAM SLOANE KENNEDY

431 Stevens st   Camden N J

thanks for your brief, flashing, indirect glances on me — not so *indirect either*

   April 13 [*1883*] — *Afternoon* —Your "Holmes" rec'd[1] —thank you kindly — The brief glance over & through it I have given impresses me — what a *clean* piece of work it is —what a *presentable* book — — Dr R M Bucke of Canada has just finished the printing (type-setting) of his book "Walt Whitman" — to be published here ab't end of this month by David McKay, 23 south 9th Phila. — (pub'r of my books) I will send you one soon as it is out — I am well, for me — have had a pretty good winter.

Walt Whitman

POSTCARD TO WILLIAM SLOANE KENNEDY

Camden   May 26 [1883]

   I congratulate you on the on the live and telling piece in to-day's C.[1]   It is the best paper that has appeared at any time in that Weekly — —I am well —

W W

[1] William Sloane Kennedy, *John Greenleaf Whittier* (Boston, 1882).

[1] William Sloane Kennedy, *Oliver Wendell Holmes* (Boston, 1883).

[1] William Sloane Kennedy, "The Obsolescence of Barrel-Organ Poetry," *Critic*, III, 239-240 (May 26, 1883).

POSTCARD TO WILLIAM SLOANE KENNEDY

Camden   May 31 '83

The publisher having placed a few advance copies in paper of Dr Bucke's W W. at my disposal I send you one The book will be pub: here & in London in abt ten days — May-be you could find a market (in some remunerative quarter) for some early notices of same — yours of 27th recd — I don't think you appreciate the importance of that article of yours, (statement, position, signal for advance &c) in the *Critic*. It entails on you deep responsibilities, & great wariness & determination in keeping it up. I mean exactly what I said in my last.

W W

TO THOMAS NICHOLSON

Camden New Jersey U S A
Evn'g Sept: 5 '83

Tommy your letter come to hand this evening, & I will just scratch off a few lines to answer at once — for I am ever so glad to know you have not forgot me, as I have not you Tommy boy. I heard by some London boy I met quite a while ago that you was married & I supposed since you had your hands full of business, new associations &c. Tom I will just tell you about things — I still live in the same quarters in Camden, but shall soon break up permanently from here. I keep pretty well — feel as well as when I last saw you, & I suppose look ab't the same —(perhaps grayer & redder) — — though young enough *in spirit* & now in my 65th year, I could easily pass for 75 or 80. — Ups and downs of course, but I thank God I have had two pretty good years — — & especially this past summer (which has been a remarkably fine one here.) — My two books bring me in a moderate income — I am satisfied with

very plain living — & bless the Lord I am likely to have
enough for that as long as I need — — Tom give my best
regards to your wife, for all I have no acquaintance with her
yet — — I wish to be remembered to any of the Asylum
boys I knew there who yet remain — I remember well the
kindness of them all, & the gay old rides around — Tom
do you recollect that Sunday evening you drove the women
in town to church, & we had a sociable drive all around ? —
that was the time we first got acquainted — I have been
thinking a good while of coming on to visit Dr Bucke again,
& then I will come & see you — God bless you Tommy
boy — your old friend,

Walt Whitman

To Charles W. Eldridge[?]

328 Mickle street
Camden   New Jersey
May 7 '84

Charley you would do me a special service if you could
get & send me a good photo (or other picture) of *Father
Taylor,* the *old sailor* preacher. I want it to be engraved
for a magazine article — Picture will be returned — also
find out for me when Father T died —
—No particular hurry —but hope you will be able to
help me soon as convenient —
— I have had a bad spell nearly all the year — till ab't a
month ago — when things turn'd favorably, & I am now
about as usual with me —

with good old remembrances
Walt Whitman

To Robert Underwood Johnson

> 328 Mickle street
> Camden New Jersey
> August 4 1884

Dear Sir

In answer to your letter[1] & request a few days ago *Yes* I will gladly write for the *Century* an article on the Hospitals & Hospital Nursing of the Secession War,[2] such as outlined by you — I will set about it immediately —
— I enclose a short sketch & reminiscence of *Father Taylor* with authentic portrait, (given me by his daughter) The price is $50[3] — If you use it I would want to see proof, & would like to reserve the right of printing it in future book — say after the lapse of a year — Respects to Watson Gilder[4]

> Walt Whitman

Postcard to William Sloane Kennedy

Camden   Sunday Evn'g Aug 10 [1884]

The *Wonders*[1] &c has arrived safely — & thank you for sending it — I am getting along pretty much in the old way — only an extra lameness —Love to you & Mrs: K —

> W. W.

Postcard to William Sloane Kennedy

> 328 Mickle street
> Camden New Jersey — Jan 8 '85

welcome Letter — return'd books, &c. just rec'd (with

---

[1] Johnson's letter is printed in *Traubel*, II, 218. A draft of the present letter is in the Library of Congress.

[2] "Army Hospitals and Cases," *Century Magazine*, XXXVI, 825-830 (Oct., 1888).

[3] "Father Taylor and Oratory," *ibid.*, XXXIII, 583-584 (Feb., 1887).

[4] Gilder's letter of acceptance appears in *Traubel*, II, 212.

[1] William Sloane Kennedy, *Wonders and Curiosities of the Railway* (Chicago, 1884).

slip — thanks) — Am feeling well — Fine & sunny to-day
— Have had a pleasant two-hours visit from Edmund
Gosse[1] —

Walt Whitman

POSTCARD TO WILLIAM SLOANE KENNEDY

328 Mickle st Camden N J
June 10 '85

Dear K   I return the MS —It has a magnificence of
strength, originality & suggestion — & I adhere fully to
what I advised in my former note —   I think a synopsis of
V. H. and T. with — [the other party] — & then this MS.
brought in as the reason for being   synopsis[1] writing — just

?

the same as Homer compiles the first 18 books of the Iliad,

purely to bring in the remaing 6 $\dfrac{\text{the main}}{\text{matter}}$ W W

POSTCARD TO EDWARD CARPENTER

Camden New Jersey U S America

Aug 5 '85 — I wrote to you a few days since acknowledging
with deepest thanks yours of June 9, safely rec'd — &
stating that I had been prostrated by the heat, somewhat
badly, but was on the mend. — I still hold my own & consider myself recuperating — —I hope you will meet my
young American lady friend Mary Whitall Smith at Mrs.
Gilchrist's — W W

---

[1] This visit, on January 3, 1885, is described in Edmund Gosse, *Critical Kit-Kats* (New York, 1896), pp. 100-107.

---

[1] In *The Poet as a Craftsman* (Philadelphia, 1886), Kennedy discusses Victor Hugo and Tennyson, and concludes with Whitman. This comparison was suggested by Whitman (Oral S. Coad, "Seven Whitman Letters," *Journal of the Rutgers University Library*, VIII, 18, Dec., 1944). The brackets around "the other party" are Whitman's.

Postcard to William Sloane Kennedy

328 Mickle street
Camden New Jersy Aug: 5 [1885]

Your card rec'd some days since —I had a sun stroke two weeks ago —makes me weak since (legs and bones like gelatine) — but I guess I am recuperating —My Phila: publisher McKay was just over here to pay me the income on the last six months' sales of my two Vols. L of G. and S Days —the am't was $22: & six cts.[1]

W W

Postcard to William Sloane Kennedy

328 Mickle street   noon
Camden   New Jersey   Aug: 10 '85

Dear W S K — Just rec'd your cheering letter —with contents — all safe. Thanks — I am getting along but lack any thing like strength or alertness — No probability of my visiting Boston — pleasant weather as I write seated here & my little canary bird singing away like mad.

Walt Whitman

Postcard to William Sloane Kennedy

Camden New Jersey
April 17 [1886]—noon — I have rec'd the *Indexes* — thanks — I send you a paper — I read my *Death* of *Abraham Lincoln* screed in Phila: Thursday last — best turn out & most profit to me yet.[1] — I am about as usual —but certainly gradually slipping down every year. Dr Bucke has gone to England for two months. Love to you

W W

---

[1] The royalty statement, dated July 1, 1885, is in the University of Pennsylvania Library.

[1] The receipts of this lecture amounted to $692 (*Donaldson*, p. 107).

Postcard to William Sloane Kennedy

328 Mickle st.
Camden New Jersey
April 27, p m '86

I send you Dublin magazine with an article in you may like to run your eye over[1] — — After you are through with it, mail to Wm D O'Connor, Life saving service, Washington, D C — — I am ab't as usual — went down to the sea-shore three days since & had a rousing dinner of shad & Champagne with some friends — W W

Postcard to William Sloane Kennedy

328 Mickle street
Camden   May 4 [1886] p m

The wine has arrived, — has been tried, & proves delicious —best & many thanks — — warm, dry, growing weather here — —I am going out for a two-hours evening drive —go out most every day —Dr Bucke is in England ——Burroughs is going to jaunt through Kentucky.
                                                    W W

To Wlliam Sloane Kennedy

Camden —   June 17 [1886] — p m
I have rec'd the Ruskin "Art" booklet[1] — thanks — — Am ab't as usual in health — hot weather here to-day
                                                    W W

Postcard to William Sloane Kennedy

Camden   June 23d [1886] — p m
When you address me, always write the *New Jersey* out

[1]H. Rowlandson's review of Edward Carpenter's *Towards Democracy* appeared in the *Dublin University Review*, II, 319-328 (April, 1886).

[1] *Art and Life: A Ruskin Anthology*, comp. William Sloane Kennedy (New York, 1886).

in full on envelope   I am not at all afraid of my handwriting apearing on the printer's copy — Yours of 21st
rec'd — acknowledging mine contain'g note of introduction
to Symonds.[1] I suppose you rec'd the big MS. of yours, (con-
cordance of criticisms &c)[2] — I *returned some ten days ago*
— but you havn't acknowledged it —all right & satisfactory
the way you propose.   Take your time, & follow out &
fulfil what the spirit moves you to make.   I will authenticate statistics &c   W W

Postcard to William Sloane Kennedy

328 Mickle street
Camden New Jersey
July 30 '86 — a m

Yes, I am ready for the MS[1] — Send it on.

W W

Postcard to William Sloane Kennedy

328 Mickle street
Camden   Aug: 4 [1886] — noon —

Your MS book has not arrived yet — I am ab't as usual —
Cool & sunny weather as 1 write —

W W

[1] This letter is in the collection of Edward Naumberg, Jr., New York,
N. Y.
[2] The first draft of Kennedy's *The Fight of a Book for the World* (William Sloane Kennedy, *The Fight of a Book for the World*, West Yarmouth,
Mass., 1926, p. xii).

[1] This is probably another draft of the book mentioned in the postcard of
June 23, 1886.

Postcard to William Sloane Kennedy

328 Mickle street
Camden New Jersey
Aug 4 [1886]—Evn'g — The MS Book has reach'd
me safely — I will read it at once —will carefully have an
eye to it —

W W

To William Sloane Kennedy

Camden,　　　　　　　　　　　　　　Aug 5 '86
I have looked over the 2d piece "Jay Charleton's" —
& it is the silliest compound of nonsense, lies & rot I have
ever seen. — Not a line but has an absurd lie —The paper
of Conway is not much better — — If you want to keep your
book from *foulness* & ridiculous misstatements you had better leave both pieces out.[1]

W. W.

Postcard to William Sloane Kennedy

Camden N J　　　　　　　　　　　　　　　4½ p m
Aug: 13 [1886] — I have just sent the MS book package to Adams' Express office, en route for Belmont — —
You ought to get it by Monday 16th — We are having a hot
spell here, & it pulls me down — W. W.

To William Sloane Kennedy

Camden.　　　　　　　　　　　　　　Aug: 18 [1886]
—I send O'Connor's letter, with the clipping from the
Nation —if you care to look at them.　I have not heard

[1] "Pen Pictures of Modern Authors (New York, G. P. Putnam's Sons,
1882) has a reprint of Conway's *Fortnightly* (1866) article and a flashy bit
of Bohemian literature by 'Jay Charlton' about W. W., originally contributed
to the Danbury *News*. 'Jay Charlton' is a pen-name of J. C. Goldsmith. I
have a manuscript letter from Whitman to me in which he pronounces Goldsmith's sketch to be 'the silliest compound of nonsense, lies and rot I have ever
seen' " (Kennedy, *The Fight of a Book for the World*, p. 55).

whether you rec'd the MS. book — I sent it hence by Adams' Express, last Friday afternoon. I remain ab't the same in health — as I write (Wednesday forenoon) it is cloudy and sufficiently cool here, & I am sitting by the open window down stairs as usual — am comfortable. —I have of late-past— been writing several pieces (as I believe I told you before) — they are to appear in time in N A Rev: — Century —& Lippincotts[1] —have been paid for — W W

POSTCARD TO WILLIAM SLOANE KENNEDY

Camden   Aug: 19 [1886] p m
— Yours of yesterday rec'd. I approve of the Chatto & Windus plan, & of the three (or two) years guarantee. — — I am glad you are going to let me have printed proofs, (say second proofs, after the *first* is read by copy & corrected) & shall count on receiving them — All ab't same as usual with me   W W

POSTCARD TO WILLIAM SLOANE KENNEDY

Camden   Tuesday p m
                                              Sept 7 [1886]
Yours rec'd.   Herbert Gilchrist's address is
                12 Well Road
                Hampstead
                London England
I am ab't as usual —Fine weather here—(to-day a little warmer.)   I send a paper — W W

POSTCARD TO WILLIAM SLOANE KENNEDY

Camden   Sept 14 [1886]
Know nothing of such an issue of L of G by any "antique

[1] "Some War Memoranda — Jotted Down at the Time," *North American Review*, CXLIV, 55-60 (Jan., 1887); "Father Taylor and Oratory," *Century Magazine*, XXXIII, 583-584 (Feb., 1887); "My Book and I," *Lippincott's Monthly Magazine*, XXXIX, 121-127 (Jan., 1887).

bookseller" in Boston[1] —Doubt if it is worth tracing out, or noting —All goes on with me much the same — — perfect weather here — I have been reading Cowley —well pleased — W W

Postcard to William Sloane Kennedy

328 Mickle street
Camden N J Oct: 16 '86
P M

Yours of 14th rec'd by mid-day mail — *Good roots* (as the N Y boys used to say) *to your venture* — I havn't heard from O'C. in quite a while —I fear he is medically in a bad way — I am sailing along ab't as usual — have just had my light dinner — Cool & raw weather here — —my canary is singing blithely as I write — Walt Whitman

Postcard to William Sloane Kennedy

Camden   Dec. 23 [1886]

I send you three little French pamphlets & one Scotch — When through reading them (no hurry) send the whole to Wm D'O Connor, Life saving service, Washington D C— I am ab't same as usual again — Merry Christmas to you & Mrs. K   Walt Whitman

Postcard to William Sloane Kennedy

Camden   Dec. 28 '86

I am ab't as usual & in good spirits & condition — Have been out driving to-day, & have eaten a good dinner (oysters &c) — Have a Tennyson *blaat* in the forthcoming Critic of Dec. 31[1] —Happy New Year!

Walt Whitman

[1] For additional information about this proposed issue of *Leaves of Grass*, see pp. 74-75.

[1] "A Word about Tennyson," *Critic*, N.S., VII, 1-2 (Jan. 1, 1887).

Postcard to William Sloane Kennedy

Camden — Jan 26 '87.

Your card acknowledging paper came — Sylvester Baxter (back'd by Mr Lovering) opened the pension proposal five weeks ago —I immediately wrote to S B positively prohibiting it —the next thing I hear of is Mr. L's bill[1] —I have finally concluded to let the thing take its course —I do *not* expect the bill to pass — I am ab't as usual — a bodily wreck — did you get "My Book & I" slip?[2] W W

To William Sloane Kennedy

Camden Feb. 21 '87 p m

Dear W S K —yours of 19th came (always welcome) with Rhys's letters (herewith returned) & the *Transcript* — Thanks —for your warm words, y'r affectionate personal & literary extra appreciation — always thanks for writing & sending —I am kept in here quite all the time & was glad you sent R's letters — Poor dear noble O Connor's ailment is I fear *locomotor ataxyia* — induration of the spine —I have heard nothing further — time only can decide —but I have serious apprhensions

— Nothing new with me — am glad your book over there is under Ernest Rhys's management & overseeing — He makes the impression on me of a deep true friend of L of G & of myself. — What is that ab't Trowbridge? I do not understand. — Had a drive yesterday thro' a splendid snowstorm — Walt Whitman

Postcard to William Sloane Kennedy

Camden Feb 22 '87 — noon

Nothing further from O'Connor See pp. 39 and 40 in

---

[1] The proposal for Whitman's pension (49th Congress, 2d Session, House Report No. 3856, Feb. 1, 1887) was withdrawn.

[2] An offprint of the article in *Lippincott's Monthly Magazine*, XXXIX, 121-127 (Jan., 1887).

Dr Buckes book ab't the wife & their hospitality to me— — they had two children, a boy died in early childhood —the girl died not long since, aged 22 or 3 —a fine girl — I knew her quite well —I cant get over what you say ab't Trowbridge — tell me the particulars — I am sitting here in the little front room writing this   Walt Whitman

To William Sloane Kennedy

Camden   March 1 '87
                                                                        2½ p m

Your letter of Sunday has come, & I am glad to get those impromptu well filled yellow sheets — *write again* — I have not heard any more from O'Connor — when I do I will tell you —I write or send papers or something every day. — Have just had my dinner — a great piece of toasted Graham bread salted & well buttered with fresh country butter, & then a lot of good panned oysters dumped over it, with the hot broth — — then a nice cup custard & a cup of coffee — So if you see in the paper that I am *starving* (as I saw it the other day) understand how — I enclose Rhys's letter rec'd this morning —As I understand it, Wilson is no more in the W & McC.[1] partnership Glasgow but sets up by himself — Walt Whitman

Postcard to William Sloane Kennedy

Camden   March 9 [1887] noon
Much the same with me.   No further news of O'Connor. (I forward the "Transcripts" you send me, to him.)   Rhys writes me that the Walter Scott, Eng: pub's will bring out my "Spec: Days" in one vol. & "Dem: Vistas. &c" in another. I have just sent on a little preface to S D. I forward a Peora paper — when you have read it, mail to Dr Bucke.

[1] Wilson & McCormick, publishers.

I have just had an autograph hunter visitor, but with cheery talk and presence.

Walt Whitman

POSTCARD TO WILLIAM SLOANE KENNEDY

Camden   Wednesday 12:40   p m [April 13, 1887]
Am feeling fairly —Start in some three hours in the train for New York —to lecture to-morrow afternoon[1] — — Return here Friday —

Walt Whitman

POSTCARD TO WILLIAM SLOANE KENNEDY

New York   —Westminster Hotel
April 15 [1887] – a m —All went off smoothly — Lincoln lecture yesterday afternoon, (good audience) & reception last evening.   — I return to Camden this afternoon —

Walt Whitman

POSTCARD TO WILLIAM SLOANE KENNEDY

328 Mickle street
Camden N J April 19 '87
Am here in my little old shanty again, & every thing ab't as usual —Stood it very well in N Y — it was a good break f'm my monotonous days here, but if I had stayed long, I sh'd have b'n killed with kindness & attention — — I rec'd $250 — Yr's just come. Thanks—Walt Whitman

POSTCARD TO WILLIAM SLOANE KENNEDY

Camden   April 20 [1887] noon
Thank you specially for sending me the Mrs Gilchrist book review in Boston Herald.[1] — send one directed *Her-*

[1] On April 14, 1887, Whitman read his Lincoln lecture at the Madison Square Theatre in New York.

[1] "Memoirs of Anne Gilchrist," *Sunday Herald* for April 17, 1887.

bert H Gilchrist, 12 Well Road, Hampstead, London Eng
—Fine sunshine here as I write & I am feeling well —
Walt Whitman

POSTCARD TO WILLIAM SLOANE KENNEDY

Philadephia   April 22 '87

Have come over here on a few days' visit to R P Smith
on Arch street — Enjoy all —Have just had my dinner —
— Mr S is one of my kindest friends. y'r letters rec'd —
always welcomed. The Gilchrist book[1] seems to be making
quite a ripple — Yr comments on it I tho't tip top —
Walt Whitman

POSTCARD TO WILLIAM SLOANE KENNEDY

Camden   April 29 [1887] a m

— Feeling pretty fair to-day. Drove down yesterday four
miles to "Billy Thompson's," on the Delaware river edge,
to a nice dinner, baked shad & champagne galore,[1] — —
jolly company —enjoy'd all with moderation —No, the
Mr Smith, my liberal & faithful Quaker friend is R Pearsall
Smith, (glass manufacturer & man of wealth) father of
Mrs. Costelloe, my staunchest living woman friend —the
Librarian Logan Smith, (now dead) was his brother —
Did you get the N Y. Eve. Sun of 15th Ap?[2] W W

POSTCARD TO WILLIAM SLOANE KENNEDY

Camden   May 16 [1887] Evn'g

Nothing different or new — I am so-so — up and
around — Sidney Morse from your way is here *sculping*
me — (full length, seated in big chair —goes on well so far)
— Fine weather here — I am seated near the open window

---

[1] *Anne Gilchrist: Her Life and Writings*, ed. Herbert H. Gilchrist (London, 1887).

[1] This dinner is described by James M. Scovel in *Kennedy*, pp. 15-16.
[2] "The Good Gray Poet is White Now," *Sun*, April 15, 1887. The "Librarian" was probably Lloyd Pearsall Smith.

writing this —Shall probably go out for a drive of an hour or two after supper —Walt Whitman

POSTCARD TO WILLIAM SLOANE KENNEDY

Camden   May 23 [1887]

Nothing very notable with me—Hot weather here — Sidney Morse continues *at me,* (sculping the full-length figure, big rocking chair) & seems succeeding — I am so-so in health   Walt Whitman

POSTCARD TO WILLIAM SLOANE KENNEDY

Camden   May 25 '87

Rec'd Rhys's note ab't the book & Symonds —Rec'd S B's letter & project for me —(or *your* project[1] for me) — Should gratefully accept. I am well as usual —hot here — am sitting here by the window as I write — ate my dinner with appetite — heard from O'Connor day before yesterday — news unfavorable — Whitman

POSTCARD TO WILLIAM SLOANE KENNEDY

Camden   Saturday
                                    3 p m [May 28, 1887]

Showery & coolish here the last two days —I am now sitting here by the open window — have had my dinner, eaten with relish —Sidney Morse is still here working — You shall see a photo of the figure he has made of me soon. Herbert Gilchrist is here in America The news from O'Connor is unfavorable. I suppose you rec'd the pictures I sent for Mrs. F.[1]   Walt Whitman

POSTCARD TO WILLIAM SLOANE KENNEDY

Camden   New Jersey

June 3 [1887]— p m —Yours of June 1 rec'd this

---
[1] Note by Kennedy: "The Timber Creek Cottage Project."

[1] Elizabeth Fairchild.

afternoon — Thanks — best & joyfulest thanks to you & Baxter & all — I will write to you to-morrow, (or next day) after thinking it over a bit, & tell you detailedly —at present I have not settled on *spot* — but am fill'd with gratitude & pleasure at the prospect of having a country or perhaps sea shore shanty of my own — Walt Whitman

Postcard to William Sloane Kennedy

Camden N J   June 9 [1887] Evn'g

Your card of yesterday rec'd. Best thanks — I am feeling unwell & stupid dont want to think or talk these times —shall emerge soon, & then define what I spoke of in my last card — Do *not* come on personally as that would not facilitate — My *Specimen Days in America* no "Collect" is out in London and a very pretty shilling Vol —with a short Pref: & add'l note for Engl: readers —I shall have some vols. & will send you one — Tell Rhys to try Sonnenschien & Co: Paternoster Sq: to publish your book — Herbert Gilchrist & Morse are here. — hot to-day —Walt Whitman

To William Sloane Kennedy

Camden   Monday forenoon
                 June 13 '87

Yours of 11th just rec'd — it is a fine bright morning, just the right temperature — — I am feeling better to-day — freer (almost free) of the heavy congested condition (especially the head department) that has been upon me for nearly a week — Took a long drive yesterday & have been living much on strawberries of late —Don't write much— just sold & got the money for — & it comes in good, I tell you a poem to *Lippincotts* — (Mr Walsh editor —friendly to me) — poem called "November Boughs"[1] a cluster of

[1] "November Boughs," *Lippincott's Monthly Magazine*, XL, 722-723 (Nov., 1887).

sonnet-like bits, making one piece in shape like (Fancies at Navesink" — that "November Boughs" is the name, by the by, I think of giving my little book, I want to have out before '87 closes —shall probably print it here in Phila: myself ——it will merely give the pieces I have uttered the last five years, in correct form, more permanent, in book shape — probably nothing new. —I see a piece in Saturday's June 11 N Y *Times*[2] that Boyle O'Reilly is treasurer of my *summer cottage fund* — (dear Boyle, if you see him say I sent my best love & thanks) —I wish you fellows Baxter, Mrs. F., yourself &c to leave the selection, arrangement, disposal &c of the cottage, (where, how, &c) *to me* — the whole thing is something I am making much reckoning of — more probably than you all are aware —the am't shall be put of course to that definite single purpose, & *there* I shall probably mainly live the rest of my days —O how I want to get amid good air — the air is so tainted here, five or six months in the year, at best —As I write Herbert Gilchrist is here sketching in my portrait for an oil painting —I hear from Dr Bucke often — nothing now of late from O'Connor, who is still in So: Cal — My friend Pearsall Smith & his daughter sailed for England in the Eider last Saturday

Walt Whitman

Postcard to William Sloane Kennedy

Camden   June 20 '87

I send you an "Academy"[1] — when you read it, send to Dr Bucke — If you wish it, I will send you it is a handsome little Vol. one of Eng: pub'd "Spec. Days" Tell me in your next letter — Baxter has written me to say I can count on $800 — that 600 are already subscribed — & that he has

---

[2] "A Cottage for Walt Whitman," New York *Times*, June 11, 1887.

[1] Walter Lewin's review of the English edition of *Specimen Days* appeared in the *Academy*, No. 787, pp. 390-391 (June 4, 1887).

300 in hand which he can send me soon as I say the word. Nothing new —hot, hot here — Gilchrist, Morse, & J N Johnson here as I write — I am so-so   W W

POSTCARD TO WILLIAM SLOANE KENNEDY

Camden   July 9 [1887] p m

Yours of 7th rec'd with R's card. Tr. not rec'd — A good letter from E R to-day — J N J.[1] is certainly crazy —a cross between Zdenko (in Consuelo) & something more intellectual & infernal. — Very hot weather here, continued —I am feeling it badly —yet not so badly as you might fancy — I am careful, & Mrs Davis is very good & cute — As I write it is clouded over & begins to rain —H G is still here painting —Morse here — Walt Whitman

TO WILLIAM SLOANE KENNEDY

Camden   July 13 '87

Very hot to-day — now two weeks of it & I am pulled down by it badly — — feel it to-day worse than yet —have had a few mouthfuls of dinner, & am sitting here in my big chair —after reading your letter & O'C's to you — H G is here painting, & Morse sculping — I enclose my last little piece[1] — a slip copy — A N Y newspaper syndicate (S S McClure Tribune Building) vehemently solicited, & gave me $25 (far more that it is worth) — Then I have sent a three line piece "Twilight" ($10) to the "Century" wh-they accepted & paid for[2] — Hartman has been in Phila ten days, but returns to B —what do you think of him & his projected "society"?[3]—As I close every thing is faint & still with the heat —

Walt Whitman

[1] Note by Kennedy: "John Newton Johnson, southern planter. Bore!"

[1] A proof copy of "The Dying Veteran." The poem appeared in the Springfield *Daily Republican*, July 11, 1887.

[2] "Twilight," *Century Magazine*, XXXV, 264 (Dec., 1887).

[3] The Walt Whitman Society, proposed by Sadakichi Hartmann.

Postcard to William Sloane Kennedy

Camden   Sunday Evn'g   July 17 '87

Heat, heat, heat, night & day — I find Evn'g a great relief — have pass'd great part of to-day lying on the lounge, with a big palm-leaf fan — have read Fullerton in the Record and Mrs. E. in Herald — — best thanks to both — I suppose O'C is in Wash'n, very poorly, but have not got word thence of his arrival — I am just going to my supper (blackberries)   Walt Whitman

Postcard to William Sloane Kennedy

Camden   Monday Evn'g   July 18 '87

Am standing the weather pretty well so far — it's the hottest long spell I ever knew —I am quite comfortable as I sit here ab't sunset.

Walt Whitman

Postcard to William Sloane Kennedy

Camden   Thursday noon   Aug 4 '87

All going ab't as usual. I hear from Dr B and from Rhys. O'C is at Bar Harbor, Maine. I am feeling quite comfortable to-day. Not so hot here — S B has sent me nearly $800 for the cottage[1] — I send you two Wash'n *Stars* — send them to Dr Bucke — I am going out for a long drive this afternoon — Walt Whitman

To William Sloane Kennedy

Camden   Sept 7, [1887] Evn'g

I return S's[1] letter — All I can say ab't it is I myself like to get views from every quarter — then I go on the tack that seems *to me* rightest — As I write, it is clouding up dark for a thunderstorm. — I expect Dr Bucke to-morrow

---

[1] Baxter's letter, Aug. 2, 1887, is printed in *Traubel*, II, 378-379.

[1] John Addington Symonds's.

or next day — Morse and Gilchrist still here Walt Whitman

To WILLIAM SLOANE KENNEDY

328 Mickle street
Camden New Jersey Sept: 14 '87

I am ab't as usual — have just had my dinner a slice of cold roast beef, & a couple of cook'd apples wh- I ate with relish — Dr Bucke has been here for a week — leaves this evening — H G is here — leaves 21st on the Germanic. Nothing very new with me in literary matters — or anent — I sent a little poem to Harpers — (Alden) — but it came back, refused — this is the 4th refusal within a few months, & I shall try no more. — Phila: is all alive with the Centennial U S Constitutional commemoration, & will be thro' the week — I have been pressingly invited, but cannot go — (A crowd & hubbub are no place for me) — Fine weather here for several weeks — cloudy & rainy this week, however — I enclose J A Symonds's note — (rather flat it seems to me) — also something ab't Ruskin — How ab't the W W Society? Any thing new? —Yes, I shall send you a copy of English ed'n "Spec: Days" — Walt Whitman

To WILLIAM SLOANE KENNEDY

[October 4, 1887]
Camden   Tuesday p m

Nothing very different with me — I am just going out for a drive — Cool & bright weather — hear from Dr Bucke frequently — he is busy & well always writes me cheerily & chipper — wh- I like, for it is pretty monotonous here — have not heard from O'Connor for several weeks— suppose he is yet at Bar Harbor — & if "no news is good news" he must be on the mend, wh I deeply hope — I return

Symonds's letter herewith — the whole matter — *this*
letter & the Fortnightly note[1] — seems to me funny.
  ("Perhaps there may be bairns, kind sir
  Perhaps there may be *not*")
— yes I like the little English Spec. Days,[2] too — you
keep y'r copy — — I have a photo. for you soon too, —
One from Cox's (NY) *I* call it the laughing philosopher[3]
— W W

POSTCARD TO WILLIAM SLOANE KENNEDY

Camden   Oct: 20 '87
O'Connor has been here visiting me on his return to Wash'n
— I have written an acc't to Dr B. wh- he will send you —
I sh'd not wish any such item as that ab't my alleged opinion
of Stedman to be printed[1] — I have no such opinion —My
feeling toward S is one of good will & thanks, markedly —
O'C says he is a good fellow, & I say so too. — Nothing new
with me specially — A new little piece of mine out in Nov.
Lippincott's[2] wh- I will send you probably to-day
                                              Walt Whitman

POSTCARD TO WILLIAM SLOANE KENNEDY

Camden   Oct: 26 [1887] p m
  Y'r card of 24th rec'd — I keep on ab't as usual — please
send the O'C letter of mine to John Burroughs, West Park,
N Y — — Letters rec'd this noon from yourself, Dr B.
and J B —pleasant for me — makes up for the glum
weather — W W

[1] John Addington Symonds, "A Note on Whitmania," *Fortnightly Review*,
N.S., XLII, 459-460 (Sept., 1887).
[2] *Specimen Days in America* (London, 1887).
[3] This photograph appears in the *New England Magazine*, N.S., XX,
frontispiece (March, 1899).

[1] Sadakichi Hartmann's interview with Whitman.
[2] "November Boughs," *Lippincott's Monthly Magazine*, XL, 722-723
(Nov. 1887).

POSTCARD TO WILLIAM SLOANE KENNEDY

Camden   Nov: 16 '87

Your card rec'd — I dispatch to-day by express the plaster head, directed to *Care Sylv: Baxter Herald office, 255 Washington st. Boston.* (It ought to go through to-morrow) I also mail to you at Belmont the Cox photo. we call "the laughing philosopher". The head I want given to some appropriate permanent gallery in Boston, that you & S B decide on — W W

TO WILLIAM SLOANE KENNEDY

Camden

Nov. 17 '87 noon

I express'd the plaster head to you last evening pre-paid, address'd to you, Care of Sylvester Baxter, Herald office 255 Washington st. Boston — it is in a stout rather heavy box — I myself like the head muchly —it is what we call the 2d head — Morse made one, the 1st, with more brood-ing-repose & dignity, more of the antique spirit &c. wh-many like best — it *is* good & attractive but tho' I like the 1st decidedly I am quite clear *this* is the typical one, modern, reaching out, looking ahead, democratic, more touch of ani-mation (perhaps unsettledness) &c. &c. not intended to be polished off — left purposely a little in the rough—I sup-pose you rec'd my cards — You and S B think over what I say ab't giving the head to some Boston Art Institution or (if you prefer) other depositary appropriate. *You & he have absolute power to dispose of it in that way* — It ought to be ready for you there at the Herald office, Friday or Sat-urday morning — I also sent you by mail to Belmont the Cox photo you requested — hope you will write me Tuesday (or Wednesday) ab't all, the meeting &c. details — I am ab't as usual, health &c—pretty dull & heavy — M D Conway has been to see me—No word from O'C. Morse is here. I expect to see Ernest Rhys soon. I get word from Dr B. often. Sunshiny out to-day — I think of going forth with horse & rig after dinner God bless you and wife —

Walt Whitman

POSTCARD TO WILLIAM SLOANE KENNEDY

Camden   Nov. 29 [1887] latter p m

As I write I am sitting in my big chair — *cold* to-day here — sunny however — Morse is here working on a life size Emerson — (somewhat of a demand for them) — Your last letter good reading for him (& me too) — dont *push* the getting of the head into any Boston gallery ("wait for the wagon") — it must depend on its *artistic* merits —as a piece of modeling &c — Nothing new with me — No E Rhys yet — — I have heard from O Connor —tolerable —

Walt Whitman

POSTCARD TO WILLIAM SLOANE KENNEDY

Camden   Dec: 7 [1887] p m

Yours rec'd to-day — Rhys has arr'd & in N Y — Expect him here now every day — I have just written a few lines on Whittier (by request & moderate cash) for an illustrated Phila: periodical, wh- I will send you when printed[1] — Morse decidedly likes the Art Museum as the place to put the bust (& I am inclined the same) but as I said leave it to you & B —Affectionate regards to Mrs. Fairchild — OConnor is poorly — I had a letter from Mrs. O'C. I continue ab't the same — Write often as you can — Have Hartmann & the "Society" completely fizzled?   W W

[1] Whittier's letter, thanking Whitman for the greeting in *Munyon's Illustrated World*, is printed in *Traubel*, II, 8.

Postcard to William Sloane Kennedy

Camden   Dec. 27 '87 Evn'g

Much the same as of late with me. I was out to Christmas dinner —turkey & champagne galore—Rhys is here — Morse has gone to Richmond, Indiana — address there care of Wm B Morse — send the "Time" magazine[1] to Dr. Bucke after reading it — Walt Whitman

To William Sloane Kennedy

Camden   Jan 10 '88

Am sitting here by the fire alone early afternoon & will write you a few lines —have had my light dinner —(stew'd chicken & a cup of tea & enjoy'd with sufficient zest,) — Feelings in general not much different —of good substantial spirits, the fund still holds out — but quite a perceptible steadily almost rapidly increasing weakness of limb-strength, eyesight, &c.—In fact a, more or less slow, loosening & deadening of the physical machine — After a dark storm, (with snow,) nearly a week, the sun is out this afternoon & there is a half-thaw. —My friend Pearsall Smith (who is very kind all along,) was here yesterday & bro't a great bundle of London literary weeklies &c. wh- I have been looking over — I like the advertisement pages ab't as well as any —I suppose Ernest Rhys is there with you — I sent him three letters yesterday enveloped to your care. I rec'd your letter — Wilson then is to pub. y'r book[1] — If you think well of it, express the whole MS. first, to me here, that I may look over & authenticate — Put it in stout pasteboards tie well, & direct fully & carefully, & it will easily travel & the expense will not be great   W W

[1] Roden Noel, "Mr. Swinburne on Walt Whitman," *Time*, XVII, 653-658 (Dec., 1887).

[1] Kennedy's proposed work on Whitman.

POSTCARD TO WILLIAM SLOANE KENNEDY

Camden   Evn'g Jan 24 '88
 The MS. package has just come, all right, freight p'd
— I am perhaps better than three weeks ago —' the cold
pinches me — very cold here for over a week. — What of
Rhys? — Did he get the five letters I sent? — I have been
invited (by letter of J G B)[1] to write for the N Y Herald —
            W W

POSTCARD TO WILLIAM SLOANE KENNEDY

Camden   Jan: 26 [1888] late Evn'g
—I have look'd over the MS &c — hardly made any emendations — Shall send it back soon — Y'r card dated 24th
rec'd — What do you mean ab't E R?[1] — write more fully &
plainly — I am ab't as usual —very cold here — —It is
most 10 & I am going off to bed —   W W

POSTCARD TO WILLIAM SLOANE KENNEDY

Camden   Feb: 1 '88
 P M — I remain ab't the same as usual —Dr Bucke was
here most of yesterday — staid over in Phila: on his way to
Florida with an invalid friend — Dr B to return in ab't two
weeks — Shall return your MS. in two or three days or so
(by express to Belmont, unless you wish otherwise) — I am
writing a little for the N Y Herald *personal column* — E R
is not here yet — weather more endurable — W W

TO WILLIAM SLOANE KENNEDY

        [February, 1888]
will send the MS. back by express next Monday, 13th —
    Put down   T B Harned
     566 Federal street
      Camden   New Jersey

---

[1] James Gordon Bennett, Jr.
[1] Ernest Rhys.

as a subscriber to the book
     c o d — (or I suppose any time)

I will send some names —

Postcard to William Sloane Kennedy

Camden   Feb. 14 '88
     I send the MS. package by express to-day, prepaid,
address'd same as this card.   Dr B. is at St Augustine, Florida.   Rhys is here —(lectures to-night before the Contemporary Club, Phila) — I continue much as usual — Sunny &
comfortable weather here to-day — Your circ. appears in
N Y. *Times*[1] & in *Post* here —

                                        W W

To the Executive Committee, Contemporary Club, Philadelphia, Pa.

To Executive Committee
Contemporary Club:
     I propose the name of Thomas B Harned Counsellor at
Law, of this city, for membership in the club.[1]
                              Walt Whitman
Camden N J
Feb: 15 '88

Postcard to William Sloane Kennedy

Camden   Feb: 17 '88
     2 p m— Yours of 15th rec'd — you ought to be getting
the MS: package as I sent it by Express three or four days
ago—Nothing new or special with me — The severe cold

[1] An announcement, quoted from the *Critic*, of "Walt Whitman, the
Poet of Humanity," by William Sloane Kennedy, is in the New York *Times*,
Feb. 13, 1888.

[1] In a letter dated Feb. 28, 1945, Mr. Thornton Oakley states that the files
of the Contemporary Club contain no information concerning Harned's ad-
mission.

has pinch'd me, but the weather is pleasanter to-day — Rhys has just left here for N Y and Boston — Dr B returns from St Augustine in ab't a week. I am sitting here anchor'd in my big chair all day — write when you can — W W

Postcard to William Sloane Kennedy

Camden   March 15 '88

I continue on ab't as usual. O'C is taking massage treatment — your last *Transcript* went from me to him, & so to Dr Bucke — I still write bits for the *Herald* — they pay me quite well —& then it is a sort of spur or fillip — A fearful four-day spell of cold, snow & gale here, but I have not felt it —the sun is shining as I write —

Walt Whitman

Postcard to William Sloane Kennedy

Camden   March 22 p m '88

Yours of 21 & the *Transcripts* & the Scotch papers rec'd — thanks for all — I have written you quite copiously lately — I continue well for me — all the little *Herald* pieces will appear (with misprints corrected) in *November Boughs* — two things the reason why of this card. *Dont let your Wilson book go to press till you have read the proofs.* 2d — please enclose to me the Alabama letter to be returned to you[1] — dont mind its malignance — the blizzard & its immediate results all over here — dark and rainy now — I am sitting here alone in the big chair   W W

To William Sloane Kennedy

Camden   Evn'g March 26 '88

I return Mr Johnson's letter — I do not see any thing in it more than facts or appearances warrant — as he is & as things are down there poor J is in a bad unhappy fix —

[1] This is probably the letter from John Newton Johnson quoted in *Kennedy*, pp. 19-21.

as of coffee being ground in a mill —Much relieved to
know you will *yourself* see all the proofs of the Wilson
book — give them a good searching reading — for with
Dr Bucke's book they are to be in all probability the vignette & authority of many things in my & my works' future
—the backward & contemporary reference. Nothing new in
particular with me — more or less evidences of gradual
physical deterioration — but spirits good —appetite &c
fair — & you know I begin my 70th year now in ab't two
months —thank God indeed that things are as well as they
are & that I & my fortunes (literary & otherwise) are —
Rainy & dark & raw here all day — I was out yesterday four
hours to my friends the Harneds — was taken & bro't back
in my phaeton — a lull in my *Herald* contributions —I
send you the *Kottabos* from Dublin[1] —Morse is still out in
Indiana — Dr B kindly writes to me often & you must do so
too

> Walt Whitman

To William Sloane Kennedy

Camden
May 7 Evn'g '88

Here is Rhys's last letter to me — I suppose (but
don't know for certain) that *Union League Club New York
City* w'd reach him — I have been out driving this afternoon
& was out yesterday, wh- is the best indication I can give of
myself — I still write a little, but almost hate to not wanting
to tack on lethargy & indigestion &c to what I have already
uttered — Thank you for the Transcripts & the last Sunday
Herald—   Walt Whitman

[1] "The classical students of Trinity College, Dublin, issue (or once issued)
a periodical called *Kottabos.* Vol. 1, no. 1, 1888, has a translation . . . of . . .
Come Lovely and Soothing Death" (Kennedy, *The Fight of a Book for the
World,* p. 42).

Postcard to William Sloane Kennedy

Camden   Tuesday afternoon
                                          June 26 '88

The roses came by the mid-day mail & have been enjoy'd
hours & hours — The doctor says I certainly do not lose
hold — but I have had a very weak bad forenoon — —
the weather is hot, hot — somewhat better now & sitting up
this moment & comfortable—Walt Whitman

Postcard to William Sloane Kennedy

Camden   Wednesday Sunset
                                          July 11 '88

Am setting up & have just eat my supper — The flowers
rec'd this day —perfumed & delicious — before me this
moment — thanks to dear Mrs: K. — pretty sick yet, but
shall rally.

                                          Walt Whitman

Postcard to William Sloane Kennedy

Camden   Friday afternoon
                                          July 27 '88

No set back essentially but still imprisoned by room &
bed — sitting up most of the day. — *Nov: Boughs* is ab't
done. My head (physical brain) & spirits good — legs &
bodily strength *gone*.

                                          Walt Whitman

To William Sloane Kennedy

Camden   Saturday Night
                                          Sept: 1 '88

Dear W S K

Yours[1] came right. I am still imprison'd in my sick
room, yet sitting up & reading & writing & (in limits)

---

[1] Kennedy's letter, Aug. 30, 1888, is printed in *Traubel*, II, 243.

talking & being talked to. — It is all tedious & long drawn out — the worst no prospect of real improvement — I mean in any body or leg strength, wh' is very low indeed —but my spirits &c. sort o' fair — appetite & sleep not bad considering — — I do not want any thing, comfort or necessity, I crave for — — I shall print the little booklet *November Boughs* 140 pp. — and at same time a big Vol. (900 pages) comprehending *all* my stuff — verses & prose — bound in one — —Shall send you copies soon as ready — will be a few weeks yet — I hear from Dr B, O'C, and J B — I get the *Transcripts* & thank for them — Traubel is unspeakably faithful & kind[2]— W W

Postcard to William Sloane Kennedy

Camden   Wednesday p m
                                                    Sept: 19 '88

Y'r letter arrives   Still here in my sick room.   I sit up — occasional visitors — -bad weather lately — I rec'd a note from Rolleston (Ireland) that he had got first proofs of the German trans of L of G[1] — I sent word to Dr Knortz but no answer comes — I get word often from Dr Bucke — the printing of *November Boughs* and the complete Vol. proceeds fairly — I am feeling satisfactory.   H. Gilchrist here yesterday — Walt Whitman

Postcard to William Sloane Kennedy

Camden   Tuesday Evn'g
                                                    Oct: 16 '88

Thanks for the *Thackeray* pamphlet, (wh' I have been reading through this afternoon)[1] —& the *Transcripts* —

---

[2] This is in reply to Kennedy's statement: "For some reason Mr. Traubel has never seen fit to tell me anything about your daily doings—" (*ibid.*).

[1] Walt Whitman, *Grashalme*, trans. Karl Knortz and T. W. Rolleston (Zürich, 1889).

[1] A "piece on Thackeray by Guernsey" (*Traubel*, II, 492).

Pretty much the same sing song with me —no worse —no better — I am waiting with anxiety to hear from O'C — the bad trouble with his eyesight

Walt Whitman

To William Sloane Kennedy

Camden   Friday Evn'g
Oct: 19 '88

It is dark & I have had my dinner & am sitting by the fire & gas light — anchor'd & tied in my old big democratic chair & room, the same as all summer, now in the fall & soon the long winter & (if I live) probably through all — I have been occupied most of the afternoon writing my autographs — there are to be 600 for the Edition of my complete writings — it will be ab't 900 pages, & include *all*, — a last few? revisions (no changes at all, but a few misprints, brokennesses, & errors corrected) — will be an *authenticated* ed'n — You shall have one — I will send one when ready — It is slow, but I am in no hurry. — Y'r card[1] came this p m. but no *Trans:* with notice yet[2] — (will doubtless come to-morrow.) — No further word from O'C. I wait with anxiety — I told you ab't my dear friend John Burroughs being here —he is now back at West Park — I hear from Dr B. very often — welcome letters —have been reading Ellis's "Early English Metrical Romances" (Bohn's Ed'n) — Miss Pardoe's Louis XIV, and several Carlyle books including Mrs. C's Letters — — Symonds's "Greek Poets" &c — upon the whole, get along & baffle lonesomeness, inertia & the blues. God bless you & the wife —

Walt Whitman

[1] Kennedy's card, Oct. 18, 1888, is printed in *Traubel*, II, 507.
[2] "Walt Whitman's New Volume," Boston *Evening Transcript*, Oct. 17, 1888.

POSTCARD TO WILLIAM SLOANE KENNEDY

Camden   p m Dec: 29 '88

Yr's rec'd ab't the books[1] — many best thanks — have
rec'd letters from Mrs: F and F B S acknowledg'g them.
Also from Baxter — am slowly improving probably —am
sitting here alone by oak-fire as I write —Just now comes a
letter from Harland[2] receipting his book — Tell me in y'r
next what was the express freight please — Dr B writes most
every day — O'C is poorly but gritty.

                                          Walt Whitman

To WILLIAM SLOANE KENNEDY

Camden   Saturday p m Jan: 5 '89

Nothing very notable or different.   Your letters rec'd
& welcomed *Trascripts* also — hearty thanks for y'r services
& promptness in conveying the books   Yes I will leave you
to pay express tax —but I had meant to refund — I have
rec'd from every one letters of acknowledgm't &c.   (Mrs:
Fairchild's to you is here enclosed return'd) Baxter's splendid
notice & setting-forth of the book, in *Herald* of last Thursday[1] is rec'd, & seems to me the most complete & most
friendly & penetrating (from the point of view of an ab-
sorber, believer & democrat) I have ever had — Dr Bucke
will have a good time over it — I hear from B often — he
is well busied with his large family, with the Asylum, &
with that *meter invention*[2] I suppose you have heard of.

[1] Whitman sent five copies of *Complete Poems & Prose* ([Camden], 1888)
to Kennedy for distribution to Garland, Baxter, F. B. Sanborn, and Mrs. Fairchild.   The fifth copy was for Kennedy (*Traubel*, III, 314, 348).

[2] Hamlin Garland: "—he always gets the name wrong — speaks of it as
a 'perverseness' " (*Traubel*, III, 406).

[1] Baxter's review appeared in an early edition of the Boston *Herald*, Jan.
3, 1889.

[2] "Bucke very often spoke of the water meter.   It was invented by William
Gurd, Mrs. Bucke's brother.   It was never put on the market commercially.
. . . Dr. Bucke probably assisted in a financial way to its invention but did not
go very deeply financially into the matter" (letter from Edwin Seaborn, Dec.
7, 1944).

O'Connor keeps on, but is badly off I fear. Burroughs is pretty well —We have had a long stretch of the finest weather, but to-day is dark & wet & glum enough — but I feel comparatively comfortable. I live on mutton-broth & milk & dry toast — sit up most of the day — have read Tolstoi & (it seems to me) all Carlyle's letters —& have enough. Much obliged with the *Trans.* ¶ on big book[3]

Sunday, Jan: 6 — All continues well —glum weather however. I am sitting here by the oak fire comfortable —

Walt Whitman

To John W. Tilton

Camden New Jersey
Jan: 6 '89

Yr's[1] of 3d recd here. The big book "Complete Works" &c: is $6. It contains "Democratic Vistas" — With four portraits extra on loose sheets it w'd be $6.50 — If you desire it, send p o money order —& send word whether you prefer by mail or express

Walt Whitman

I can send in a little paper bound Vol: "Dem: Vistas" — 50cts — if wanted

Postcard to William Sloane Kennedy

Camden   Jan: 22 [1889]

Don't hurry ab't sending the French magazine to Dr B — — Do you read French? —If entirely convenient, give me a brief resumé of it, the Sarrazin piece[1] (or the am't of

---

[3] "Walt Whitman's Complete Works," Boston *Evening Transcript*, Dec. 29, 1888.

[1] John W. Tilton (1844-1917), of Haverhill, Mass., lawyer and book collector.

[1] Gabriel Sarrazin, "Poètes modernes de l'Amérique: Walt Whitman," *La Nouvelle Revue*, LII, 164-184 (May 1, 1888). Whitman had abstracts by Kennedy and Bucke set up in type (Kennedy, *The Fight of a Book for the World*, p. 46).

it) when you write again — Who wrote that notice first page last *Critic*?[2] It penerated & pleas'd me much.

Walt Whitman

Postcard to William Sloane Kennedy

Camden   Evn'g Feb: 14 '89
I've sent a Sarrazin to Baxter & to Harland.

Yr's came to-day welcome —I send "Magazine Poetry"[1] only half thinking it may be a sort of curiosity to you —Mail it to Dr B as he owns it & wants it back —O'C is still roomfast & badly off — I am fearful of the worst luck (of wh- a long miserable helpless lingering condition is perhaps worst) — sunny & cold here — I am ab't as usual a cold in the head — Walt Whitman

Postcard to William Sloane Kennedy

Camden   Feb: 24 '89
The "Magazine of Poetry" reach'd Dr B all right — I expect him here by Wednesday next — (he expects to practically start that *meter* company & manufacturing) — O'C is still very ill — he is yet eager that his late essay backing the pro-Bacon anti-Shaksperean argument shd be publish'd — I hope so too — — Nothing very new with me — Am somewhat worse, (side-pains day & night) — There is a good notice in London *Pall-Mall* Jan: 25[1] Sunny & very cold here — Walt Whitman

Postcard to William Sloane Kennedy

Camden   Feb: 25 '89
Yours of 22d rec'd — I send the little German trans:.

---

[2] "Walt Whitman's 'November Boughs,'" *Critic*, N.S., XI, 25 (Jan. 19, 1889).

[1] Richard Maurice Bucke, "Walt Whitman," *Magazine of Poetry*, I, 15-23 (Jan., 1889).

[1] "The Gospel According to Walt Whitman," *Pall Mall Gazette*, Jan. 25, 1889.

from Zurich[1] — (At y'r leisure, give me a sort of English abstract of Knortz's and Rolleston's prefaces in front) — I am quite unwell — Dr B will probably be here to-morrow evn'g — I have rec'd a letter f'm Sarrazin Paris — he has the big "complete" book — — his book (with L of G. &c article) will be out soon & he will send me one, wh- I will lend you — I suppose you rec'd the Dr B trans: of S I sent[2]

Walt Whitman

POSTCARD TO WILLIAM SLOANE KENNEDY

Camden   Feb: 28 '89

The word f'm O'C to-day is more favorable — has at times the use of his eyes — can eat & keep his food — & some general "let up" — Dr B is here full of the water - meter enterprise — Keeps him busy enough (that's what he came for) —So so with me — pain steady left side — (spleen trouble Dr says) — I suppose you rec'd the German "Grashalme"

Walt Whitman

POSTCARD TO WILLIAM SLOANE KENNEDY

Camden   Evn'g   March 17 '89

Matters not very different — the *Transcripts* rec'd — read & sent to O'Connor —O'C had a very bad spell ag'n since I wrote you ab't him (epileptic fits) —but was better three days ago, but weak & in bed — Dr B here yet — — I sit here alone same as ever, in my big old chair with the thick wolf-skin back — Mrs Spaulding call'd to-day.

Walt Whitman

[1] Walt Whitman, *Grashalme*, trans. Karl Knortz and T. W. Rolleston.
[2] This article by Sarrazin is also mentioned in the postcard of Jan. 22, 1889.

POSTCARD TO WILLIAM SLOANE KENNEDY

Camden   March 22 '89

Sunny & beautiful to-day here. I am fairly well considering —News *not* of favorable or improving character
from O'C —has great weakness & fits of vomiting — Dr B
has got safely home in Canada & resumes his work —the
meter project will yet be launched, & go —the last Vol.
4th American Supplement to *Enc: Brit:* page 772 has a
notice &c of me   W W

POSTCARD TO WILLIAM SLOANE KENNEDY

Camden   April 7 '89

Much the same with me (a long bad cold in the head)
I hear often from Dr B. —The latest news from O'C is of
being a little easier —(but he is very ill) — Rough weather
here — Walt Whitman

POSTCARD TO WILLIAM SLOANE KENNEDY

Camden   April 16 '89

Nothing very different or new in my affairs — the past
ten days bad rather — sort of suspicion of lull to-day —
Y'r last rec'd — have no opinion or comment or suggestion
to make —did you receive (& send on to O'C) my letter with
Stedman's enc'd? — Am sitting here alone as usual.

                                       Walt Whitman

POSTCARD TO WILLIAM SLOANE KENNEDY

Camden   April 25 '89

Y'r card just rec'd — papers come regularly — thanks
— Nothing very different with me — Still imprison'd — my
dilapidation not mending (slowly gradually worse if any
thing, but not much change) — am preparing my (to me)
most satisfactory new really complete ed'n L of G. including
"Sands" and epilogue "Glance" — will send you one —

Am sitting here in the big chair sort o' comfortable — alone
all day — O'C still very sick —Dr B well & busy—
Walt Whitman

Postcard to William Sloane Kennedy

Camden   May 4 '89

Sarrazin's book has come, "La Ranaissance de la *Poésie
Anglaise* 1798-1889 — Paris — 35 quai des grandes Augustine" — 279 pp. handy beautiful French style, paper —
Nothing very different in my affairs — the N Y *Literary
News* for May has a notice[1] — did you see that infernal
farrago of my *opinions!!* in the Herald three Sundays ago
by that Japanee?[2] — S[3] is quite mad I hear — O'C is no
better.

Walt Whitman

Postcard to William Sloane Kennedy

Camden   May 8 '89

Yr's of 6th rec'd — thanks — yes, I am agreeable to
your sending S my former letter, (& rather advise it) —
Bad, bad word from O'C (f'm the wife) to day, & I am
gloomy —Dr B writes me every day & cheerily — Horace
& my nurse Ed have gone prospecting to Phila: for a strong
suitable *out-door chair* for me to be pull'd or push'd out.
Walt Whitman

To William Sloane Kennedy

Camden New Jersey   Evn'g, Oct. 7 '89

Here yet holding the fort gradually being sapp'd no
doubt but fair spirits yet — Yr's rec'd & always welcomed
(I enclose Dr Bucke's letter to me, mention'g y'r last wh-

---

[1] "Walt Whitman," *Literary News*, X, 180-181 (May, 1889).

[2] C. Sadakichi Hartmann, "Walt Whitman. Notes of a Conversation with
the Good Gray Poet by a German Poet and Traveller," New York *Herald*,
April 14, 1889.

[3] E. C. Stedman.

I lent him) —Nothing specially new or significant with my condition or literary matters — the proceedings of the Birth Day Dinner not yet bound but I believe have gone to press[1] — & I will send you one soon as ready

Walt Whitman

Postcard to William Sloane Kennedy

Camden   Oct: 13 p m '89

Nothing important —yrs' rec'd & welcomed — Dr B. writes me frequently — still anchor'd in my big chair — visitors & correspondence — inertia & lassitude & paralysis —slowly hardening & defining deafness & (more slowly) blindness — I send the little pocket-book ed'n L of G. Remember me to Baxter when you see him (& to all inquiring friends) — I keep up pretty good heart

Walt Whitman

Postcard to William Sloane Kennedy

Camden   New Jersey
Yr's of 15th comes)

Oct: 17 '89

Thanks for the nice currants (I have had some for my breakfast) & the good little calamus confections by mail. Thanks to the dear western girl   Nothing notable with me — am much the same — in good spirits — — If you come across a spare number of y'r new "Transatlantic Magazine" Boston send me — sunshiny here today

Walt Whitman

[1] *Camden's Compliment to Walt Whitman, May 31, 1889,* ed. Horace L. Traubel (Philadelphia, 1889).

To Edward Wilkins

Camden N J — U S A
Tuesday Night Dec: 31 '89

Dear Ed[1] Y'r letter came this forenoon & am glad you keep well & are satisfied at y'r occupation — No doubt it will turn out well as it is a good business & with ordinary luck will return a handsome income — & besides it is y'r own choice & satisfaction — wh- is a great point — Nothing very new or different here — If you were to come here (& pleas'd w'd I be to see you boy) now, you w'd see me seated by the oak wood fire in the big ratan chair with the gray wolf-skin spread on the back, & the same old litter of papers & MSS & books around on the floor in the same old muss — — I don't get any worse but no improvement in health or strength either —but I keep pretty good spirits & eat & sleep fairly yet Have my daily curryings, & get out often in wheelchair — Warren has had a couple or three days sickness —the doctor was a little afraid of typhoid fever, but it seems to have pass'd over, & he is getting ab't the same as before — Mrs: D is well — I send you a paper — hear from Dr B. often — he is well & busy — Warren is learning the fiddle — he is getting along well — takes lessons of Watson. Good bye for the present Ed & my remembrances & love to you boy   Walt Whitman

To William Sloane Kennedy

Camden   p m Jan 27 '90

Nothing very notable or different — *Transcripts* come promptly & safely — thanks — hear frequently f'm Dr Bucke — had the grip there largely & badly — he escapes

---

[1] In Nov., 1888, Dr. Bucke sent Wilkins, an attendant at the Asylum, to Camden as a nurse for Whitman. Wilkins remained in Camden until Oct., 1889, when he was succeeded by Warren Fritzinger, adopted son of Mrs. Mary O. Davis, Whitman's housekeeper. At that time Wilkins returned to London to study veterinary surgery.

— — Mrs O'C at Washington in same house — I told Horace to tell you *not* to send me $5 for the little ed'n L of G. as it was a present to you — I believe I have a little poemet in forthcoming *Century*[1] — the *Transatlantics* came — thanks — have been kept in doors by the bad weather— sun out this forenoon, but now dark — I sit here the same as ever, alone mostly, in the great chair — two massages or pummelings — & two meals breakfast & supper — no dinner — those four the main *breaks* of the day — — blessedly so far appetite, sleep, even heart, &c: continuing fair as before — but the old machine the body & brain well shatter'd & gone (that secession war experience was a *whack* or series of whacks irrecoverable) — have sold a big book & sent it off to Chicago to day — —have been out to-day in wheel-chair a short jaunt, — Lord bless you all

Walt Whitman

POSTCARD TO WILLIAM SLOANE KENNEDY

Camden   Feb: 10 '90

Y'r p c rec'd & welcomed — weather fast & room-fast here — (altho' the sun is shining out to-day) — Nothing special in my condition or affairs — — Am writing a little bits, poemets &c   I suppose to while away time as much as any thing else.   Hawser'd here by pretty short rope.   rec'd the $5 you sent — but had sent you word *not* to —all right now tho — it is ab't sundown —I am waiting for my supper — My young nurse is down stairs learning his fiddle lesson — have had my massage   Walt Whitman

TO EDWARD WILKINS

Camden   March 20 '90

Dear Ed   Yr's came this morning & welcome   Nothing very

[1] "Old Age's Ship and Crafty Death's," *Century Magazine*, XXXIX, 553 (Feb., 1890).

different here — much the same with me in health &c: am feeling at the best I am capable of these times (& that is poor enough) — had a fresh egg & nice biscuit & coffee for my breakfast — sleep fairly yet — Warren is still with me & is very kind & good — gives me first rate massages, (twice a day) — Harry[1] is quite unwell —the stomach seems to have given out, obstinately & badly, & there are other bad features — but H is young, good-spirited, & the spring of year is at hand — all favorable points to threaten'd or incipient sickness — Mrs: D is well & smiling as usual —all send love & best remembrance to you —as I do too — — I send the Camden "Morning News" of this mn'g wh- has a piece ab't me — the English register'd envelope, tho' common enough, will be one of the curios for y'r stamp collection — Ed the little dinner b'k is a present to you, & is *not* to be paid for — —Do you remember Harry Stafford? — He is quite sick, —has fits of being out of his mind — his wife has a new baby boy — Mrs: Somers's husband is dead & buried — -a young RR friend Elwood Mills consumption was buried a few days ago   Warren's friend — —you remember Florence over in Phila? she has a fine little red-headed baby boy — So the contrast — birth & life — just here I receive a beautiful bunch of great white lilies sent me f'm Bermuda —Ed when a fellow learns he knows little or nothing in reality, the old Socratic rule was *he was beginning to learn the very best* — God bless you boy

always your friend   Walt Whitman

POSTCARD TO WILLIAM SLOANE KENNEDY

Camden   Evn'g April 1 '90
   Y'r card rec'd - thanks - fine sunny day & clear evn'g, after snow storm &c — I have *the grip* at last & quite badly - am sitting here alone in my den — nothing very new — my

[1] Harry Fritzinger, brother of Warren, and adopted son of Mrs. Davis.

eyes failing — Expect to give (& wish to) my "Death of Abraham Lincoln" memorandum April 15 in Phila: — shall have a little poemet in May *Century*[1] — Did I tell you to look at (London) *Universal Review* Feb. 15 for piece ab't me by Sarrazin?[2] Love to Mrs K. —

W W

Postcard to William Sloane Kennedy

Camden   Ev'g April 11 '90
Still the grip & badly day & night — sometimes most strangles me — I fight it as if a great serpent, worst late at night — How are you & getting along? — Astonishing one can stand when put to your trumps — Transcripts come regularly   Love to you & Mrs: K   Walt Whitman

To Joseph M. Stoddart

328 Mickle street
Camden New Jersey April 24 '90

My dear Stoddart[1]
Can you use this in the magazine?[2] It is intended to make *one page* full & square —& I shall require to see a proof beforehand —(that is indispensable.) The price is $60 & a dozen copies of the magazine number. I reserve the right of printing in future book.

Respectfully &c:

Walt Whitman

If necessary I will contract or expand it (in proof) to make the fair page

[1] "A Twilight Song," *Century Magazine*, XL, 27 (May, 1890).
[2] Gabriel Sarrazin, "Walt Whitman," *Universal Review*, VI, 247-269 (Feb., 1890).

[1] Joseph M. Stoddart, managing editor (1886-1894) of *Lippincott's Monthly Magazine*.
[2] A proof copy of "To the Sun-Set Breeze" accompanies this letter. The poem appeared in *Lippincott's Monthly Magazine*, XLVI, 861 (Dec., 1890).

To Edward Wilkins

Camden   April 29 1890

Dear boy Ed: Yr's rec'd — Enclose this little billet to Mrs: Spaulding —(I have lost the address) —Ed I feel a little easier f'm my long *grip* —just ate my supper & relish'd it — was out an hour in the wheel chair this afternoon —quite warm — Warren & Mrs. Davis well — Harry pretty well (he has sold out the grocery) Horace Traubel comes regularly — I expect Dr Bucke ab't May 12 — — my legs even a little feebler (fell down to-day) — have many visitors invitations &c (some to swell dinners) all declined with thanks & respects — — As I write it is nearly sun set (days are getting quite long here) & I am sitting up here in the old den, same old heavy timber'd cane seat chair, & pretty much the same as when you was here —

Good bye Ed for the present & God bless you boy

Walt Whitman

To William Sloane Kennedy

Camden June 18 1890

Fairly with me these days — Did I tell you my last piece (poem) was rejected by the *Century* (R W Gilder) —I have now been shut off by *all* the magazines here & the *Nineteenth Century* in England — & feel like closing house as poem writer — (you know a fellow doesn't make brooms or shoes if nobody will have 'em) — I shall put in order a last little 6 or 8 page annex (the second) of my *Leaves* of *Grass* — & that will probably be the finish — I get out almost daily in wheel chair — was out yesterday down to river shore & staid there an hour — cloudy weather now fourth day, but entirely pleasant — appetite fair — had oatmeal porridge, honey & tea for breakfast — shall probably have stew'd mutton & rice for early supper (do not eat dinner at all, find it best') — have massage every day — bath also — have a good nurse Warren Fritzinger — sell a book occasionally — get along better than you might think any how —have some pretty bad spells — some talkers bores questioners (hateful)—two splendid letters lately f'm R G Ingersoll — I enclose Dr B's, rec'd this morning — Love to Mrs: K — God bless you both —

Walt Whitman

To William Sloane Kennedy

Camden   p m [Au]g: 4 '90

Hot weather he[re,] but I am getting fairly along through [i]t — bathe often & live on bread & honey get out in wheel chair at sunset & after — get to the Delaware shore as before — the last two evenings have enjoy'd steady damp cool s w breezes very refreshing — have rec'd from Addington Symonds his two new vols: "Essays Speculative & Suggestive" —one of the essays "Democratic Art, with reference to W W" — of course the whole thing is scholarly & interesting & more — I have scribbled a brief piece anent of the Dem: Art essay & sent it to the Critic — so if they print it[1] you will see, but for a good while now all my pieces come back rejected, (the Century, Harpers, the Eng: Nineteenth Century, the Cosmopolitan &c: &c: all send my pieces back) — Horace T. is well — comes in every evn'g — is invaluable to me —I enclose Dr Bucke's last just rec'd — also other things — I am sitting here in my den in the big old rattan chair writing this — if you see Baxter tell him I have rec'd his note & entirely repudiate Hartmann's W W opinions they are utterly fraudulent   Walt Whitman

[1] "An Old Man's Rejoinder," *Critic*, N.S., XIV, 85-86 (Aug. 16, 1890).

To Edward Wilkins

Camden   New Jersey
Dec: 24 1890

Dear Ed

Yr's came this mn'g, & was welcome (& you w'd be y'rself) —I am here yet, a peg additional dropping out every successive month or so but in many things *the same subject continued* — bladder trouble & the grip (aggravated cold in the head & stomach) are the worst — but I still keep pretty fair spirits & (fortunately) a stout strong right arm considering.   Things in the house are ab't same — Mrs: D has just been in, is well — Warren has gone over to Phila —I am sitting here in the big chair with wolf skin spread over back — fine sunny day out —cold — no sleighing here —write when you can, dear boy, & I will too — God bless you —

Walt Whitman

To William Sloane Kennedy

Camden   p m Dec: 29 '90

Much *the same continued* — Dr Bucke has had a bad fall & dislocated left shoulder — makes rather light of it & will probably be in fair trim before many days — writes yet — — J M Stoddart, editor Lippincott's Magazine contemplates for the March number a picture of & articles ab't (one or two *from*) W W — speaks of it as his Whitman (proposed) number — If it suits, how w'd it do to send him that piece on Dutch points?[1] —If yes, send it on to him — I am in favor of it — I have just had an order (with the money) f'm Melbourne Australia for *four* of the big books —wh- I sent by express ($7.50) — sit here imprison'd in room — Horace Traubel faithful daily —(don't know what

[1] Kennedy's article, "Dutch Traits of Walt Whitman," appears in the *Conservator*, I, 90-91 (Feb., 1891).

I c'd do without him) — have sent a cluster of poemets (a page intended) to *Scribner's* mag — have not heard yet — Mrs O'Connor's "Brazen Android" MSS for book are yet in the hands of the Houghton house y'r city[2] — no decided answer yet — Write a little most every day — read (or rather dawdle) a good deal — Keep a good oak fire — appetite, digestion, sleep, &c: might be much worse — cold— sun shining out to day on the white snow   Walt Whitman

To ——————

Seems to me you had better take half a dozen (6) copies of the big book, complete works — See Circ: herewith. I w'd send you the six for $30 (by Ex:)
May 8 '91   Walt Whitman
                   328 Mickle st: Camden N J
no "previous letter" has come

To Edward Wilkins

Camden N J   — U S America
Sept: 30 '91 — Dear Ed: Yr's of 26th has come, & I am glad to get word f'm you after such an interval — Don't wait so long again & you yourself will always be welcome whatever happens — I still hold out here, but a peg dropping out lower every month, & before long will be dropt out for good — — hardly get out at all in the wheel chair, or any other way —not once in a month — In other respects somewhat the same — eat my two meals every day — (an egg & bread & coffee for b'kfast & four or five oysters for supper yesterday) —has been a hot season here, but clear & cool to-day — every thing & folks here much the same —Mrs. D and Warry & Harry well — Mrs. Mapes out in Atchison Kansas — Mrs. Doughty & Maggie well —Warry

[2] William Douglas O'Connor, *Three Tales* (Boston and New York, 1892).

still my nurse & satisfactory — Horace Traubel married & well —faithful as ever — So good bye for present & God bless you dear son   Walt Whitman

POSTCARD TO OSCAR TOTTIE

Camden   New Jersey
U S America

July 26 — I have to-day sent, same address as this card, my Two Volumes — Please notify me (by postal card will do) soon as they reach you[1] safely.

Walt Whitman

[1] We have been unable to identify Oscar Tottie. The present postcard is pasted on the verso of the front cover of a copy of *Leaves of Grass* (1876) inscribed to him.

Letters Written by George Washington Whitman During the Civil War

Trent Collection catalogue, page 62, number 15. The letters are addressed to Mrs. Louisa Whitman, to Thomas Jefferson Whitman, or to Walt, who kept them among his papers and endorsed the dates on a large number. They were used by the poet in preparing at least two newspaper articles: "Fifty-first New York City Veterans," published in the New York Times *for October 29, 1864; and "Return of a Brooklyn Veteran," which appeared in the Brooklyn* Daily Union *for March 16, 1865.[1]*

According to Walt's account of his brother's army career, George enlisted in the Brooklyn Thirteenth Regiment in April, 1861, and after the expiration of his term of one hundred days joined the Fifty-first New York Volunteers, then commanded by Colonel Edward Ferrero, who promptly made him a sergeant major. During the early campaign in North Carolina he was promoted to the rank of second lieutenant and after the battle of Antietam, in·1862, was made a first lieutenant. As a result of gallantry in action in the first battle of Fredericksburg, during the course of which he was slightly wounded, he was elevated to the rank of captain. In his article on his veteran brother Walt wrote, with justifiable pride:

He has been in twenty-one general engagements or sieges, most of them first class of war, and skirmishing, &c., almost beyond count; has sailed the sea in long and severe storms, fought all over the blood-reddened soil of Virginia and Western Maryland, also in the Carolinas, also in Kentucky and Tennessee, also in Mississippi at Vicksburg and Jackson; and in all the Titanic

[1] The former is reprinted in *Uncollected*, II, 37-41; the latter in *Glicksberg*, pp. 85-89.

struggle of the Wilderness, and so to Petersburg and the Weldon road. He has marched across eighteen states, traversing some of them across and back again in all directions. He has journeyed as a soldier, since he first started from this city, over twenty thousand miles; and has fought under Burnside, McClellan, McDowell, Meade, Pope, Hooker, Sherman and Grant.[2]

On September 30, 1864, George, who was acting lieutenant colonel of his regiment, was captured near Poplar Grove Church, in Virginia, suffered the horrors of Libby and other prisons, and was eventually exchanged, arriving at Annapolis in February, 1865. Walt, of course, did all in his power to expedite the release of his brother, using all the influence he possessed, and even writing letters to the press, among them one to the Brooklyn Eagle *for December 27, 1864, calculated to arouse public indignation at the delay in effecting the exchange of the wretched captives.[3] After a furlough spent at home in Brooklyn, George returned to his army duties, was promoted to the rank of major, and was mustered out of service on July 25, 1865. Few veterans of the Civil War had seen more action than he.*

Most of his letters in the Trent Collection deal with his activities as a soldier or with the state of his family's health or finances. The few which have been selected for reproduction here will, it is hoped, reveal something of the loyal spirit of the man.

It may be helpful to the reader to be reminded that during the war Mother Whitman with her afflicted son Edward was living in a house on Portland Avenue, Brooklyn, which was shared by a family named Brown and by the Thomas Jefferson Whitmans. Jeff's wife, Martha ("Mattie" or "Mat"), was the mother of Mannahatta ("Hattie" or "Sis") and of

[2] *Glicksberg*, p. 89. According to the records in the Adjutant General's office, George Whitman was enrolled on Sept. 13, 1861, and was discharged on July 25, 1865. On March 13, 1865, he was appointed lieutenant colonel by brevet.

[3] Reprinted in *Glicksberg*, pp. 178-180.

California (later named Jessie), born in 1863. The fact that she seems to have been unable to relieve her mother-in-law of many household tasks is explained not only by the presence of children in her home but by her activities as a seamstress, for Jeff's income was very small.

Other members of the family mentioned in the letters are Jesse ("Jess"), the oldest brother; Mary, the older sister; Hannah ("Han"), the favorite of the family, then living in Burlington, Vermont, with her artist-husband, Charles L. Heyde; and Andrew ("Bunkum"), married to Nancy, who served for a few months as a soldier but who suffered from a throat ailment which caused his death in December, 1863. Heyde, it is apparent, was heartily disliked by all of the Whitmans, who believed that he was mistreating his wife.

On the Potomac River Near the Villiage
of Antietam Md Sunday Sept 21/62

Dear Mother

I had just commenced to write you a letter the day before yesterday when the order was given for our regt to fall in for an advance, and I had only time to let you know that I was alive and well when I had to stop writing and get ready to move.

I told you in the letter I wrote from Washington something about the battles of Bull Run and Chantilly and as I would much rather write of victories than defeats, (Although you can hardly call Chantilly a defeat as the enemy were foiled in their attempt to cut off our baggage train, though the loss on our side was heavy and included Generals Kearney and Stephens) I will tell you of what we have done for the last two weeks. We left Washington by the road leading to Frederick Md, on Sunday Sept 7th and moved by easy marches, untill Thursday Sept 11th when our advance came up with a part of the Artillery force of the enemy who were posted in a very commanding position on a range of high hills on the opposite side of a stream called the Monochey River. As soon as our advance came within range the enemy opened fire but our Artillery soon got to work throwing shot and shell so fast that the enemy were forced to leave without our Infantry being engaged at all. After the enemy fell back our forces advanced in three or four different Collumns, each takeing a different road. Our Collumn was composed of Reno's 9th Army Corps, and in the wing of the Army Commanded by General Burnside. Mc Clelan I believe was on the right of Burnside, and someone (I dont know who) was on the left. We came up with the Rebel army again on Sunday Sept 14th the enemy were posted in a splendid position on a range of Mountains Called the south Mountains or Middletown Heights. General Cox who commands a Division, of our Army Corps, somehow got around the enemy's left and drove him from his best position, on the crown of the Mountain. Our Division (which is the 2d of the 9th Army Corps and is made up princapaly of what is left of the old Burnside expedition and are commanded by General Sturgis) was then brought up and took the advance, the enemy falling back slowly untill night, when we found ourselvs, on the opposite side of the Mountains and about a mile from where the fight commenced, with all the best positions on the feild in our posession, and as it was now dark our Division formed in line of battle so as to hold all the ground we had gained during the day and lay down to await the movements of the enemy. Our Regt lay in an open field near the edge of a wood into which the enemy had been driven, and had just got our position and laid down, when the enemy opened fire on us from the woods directly in front of us. Our regt was ordered to lie close and not fire a shot untill the enemy advanced out of the woods and into the field where we lay. The regts on our right and left had a regular cross fire on the enemy and kept pouring the lead into them like rain. I had command of our Company (as the Captain was not well although he was on the field) and I had mighty hard work to keep some of them from getting up and blazing away as they said they did not like to lay there like a lot of old women and be shot without fighting back. I thought it was mighty singular myself but when I saw next morning how things were situated, I saw that as long as we lay down their fire could not harm us much, while if they had come out to the open field we would have got up and given them a volley that would have done terrible execution. The enemy kept up a sharp fire for about half an hour (and it was about the toughest half hour that I ever experianced as I could hear the bullets whiz all around me and some of them seemed to almost graze me) when the enemys fire began to slacken and it was evident that he did not intend to come out of the woods so that we could get a fair chance at him, the order was given for us to open fire and you never saw men go to work with a better relish. In about 15 minutes the enemys fire ceased altogather and we knew he had fell back out of range so we ceased fireing and lay down again untill daylight when we found there was no enemy in sight they haveing Skedadled during the night. After assuring ourselvs that they were gone for good, we stacked arms and I took a walk over our part of the battle field. In some parts of the feild the enemys dead lay in heaps and in a road for nearly a quarter of a mile they lay so thick that I had to pick my way carefully to avoid stepping on them. I think judging from what I saw that the enemys loss was fully 8 times as great as ours and I am told that the slaughter was equally as great on our right. General Reno was killed soon after we went into action and while he was looking at our position, He was

Brigadier general of our Brigade in the old Burnside expedition and was afterwards promoted to the command of the 9th Army Corps and was very much liked by all of us. After resting a few hours in the morning we pushed on again our Division takeing the lead and late in the afternoon of the 16th we found the enemy had concluded to made another stand at a stream about 100 feet wide called Antietam Creek. The bank on their side of the creek was very high and very steep and was covered with heavy woods which gave them a great advantage over us. It was so late in the afternoon that it was decided not to make an attack that night so we filed off into a field and stoped for the night. The only place near where we were, that our Artillery could cross was at a stone Bridge some 20 ft wide, where the enemy had made temporary breastworks of fence rails and logs behind which they could lay almost concealed from us while we would have to advance to the bridge through open fields in plain sight of them.

Early on the morning of the 17th the first and second Brigades of our Division was ordered down to take the bridge. The first Brigade was ordered to take a position, at our end of the bridge and try and drive the enemy from behind his shelter while our Brigade which is the 2d was to be held in reserve. The 1st did not seem inclined to advance to the position assigned them, but rather held back, so Burnside who was looking on ordered Sturgis to send our Brigade there saying, (so the story goes) that he knew we would take it. As soon as we were ordered to forward we started on a double quick and gained the position, although we lost quite a number of men in doing it. We were then ordered to halt and commence fireing, and the way we showered the lead across that creek was noboddys buisness. I had command of our Company again and as soon as the men got steadily settled down to their work I took a rifle from one of the wounded men and went in, loading and fireing as fast as any one. After about half an hour the enemys fire began to slacken a little, and soon the order was given for our Brigade to charge. The 51st Pennsylvania had the right of our Brigade and should have crossed first, but our boys could not wait, and with the cry of remember Reno, we started for the Bridge the 51st Penn and our Regt crossing togather. As soon as the rebels saw us start on a charge they broke and run and the fight at the bridge was ended. After we crossed we found the enemy had fell back about 1/2 or 3/4 of a mile to another range of hills where they were protected by stone fences, and the 3d Brigade of our Division and a part of the Division of General Cox were ordered to advance and engage them. They moved up and charged, driving the rebel Infantry in fine style when the enemy brough up a battery of Artillery which poured the grape and cannister into our boys so that they, were forced to fall back to our Brigade who was then acting as a reserve

Things began to look rather squally and although our Brigade, was nearly out of ammunition we were ordered to the front again. We formed line of battle and advanced over the hill untill we met the enemy who was moveing down towards us, when both parties took a position, and we went at it again for the 2d time in one day.

Our Regt fired every round of ammunition we had, and took all from the dead and wounded on the field and then we lay down as we would not leave the field untill we were ordered. We lay there about half an hour without fireing a shot which seemed to puzzle the rebels very much as they did not come any closer to us, but kept up a pretty brisk fire from where they were.

After a while another regiment was sent in to relieve us

and we were ordered back to the bridge where we were suplied with ammunition, and something to eat, and as it was almost night and the fireing had ceased on both sides, we were ordered to lay down and rest ourselvs and tired enough we was after our days work as you can imagine. The pickets on both sides kept up a stragling fire all night, and the next morning niether side seemed inclined to commence opperations, and so we remained all day each party occupying the same position they did when the fighting ceased the night before. During the day we took an account of stock, and found we had about 180 men left. One Company was away with the baggage train and we have quite a number sick in Hospital so I think that counting the sick and teamsters, Straglers, and cowards we have about 275 men left of the regt we brought from New York less than a year ago. The loss of our regt in the Sunday and Wednesday's fight was from 120 to 125 killed wounded and missing. Our Adjutant who lived in Brooklyn and was named Fowler, was killed at the bridge. Both Lieutenants in Co F which is on the right of our Co and both in Co K who was next to us on the left, was hit one was killed 2 was badly wounded an one slightly

At daylight on the morning of Sept 19th we found the enemy had left and we moved foreward about 3 miles to the Potomac River where we are now and as near as I can find out the enemy are all out of Md. Wel Mother I guess you will get tired before you get through reading this letter. You must not think strange when you do not hear from me often, for sometimes I do not get a chance to write for weeks. I received last week a letter from you dated the 7th and one from Jeff of the 8th. I was very glad to hear you are all getting along well. I hope Mother you will take good care of yourself and not worry and frett, for that troubles me more than anything else. I supose you know more about the situation of affairs than I do as I do not see the papers often, but it seems to me the rebels have been terribly cut up within the last few days and as near as I can find out they are all driven out of Md. I dont know how soon I will have a chance to send this, but I am pretty sure that we will move from here in the course of a day or two, and will probably go to Harpers Ferry so I shall have a chance to send it from there, if not before. I heard General Burnside say the other day that our regt would now have a chance to go in camp and rest awhile so I think likely we shall stay at Harpers Ferry awhile

You speak in your letter of Walts seeing the Captain of our Co at Major Le Gendre's office, it was the 1st Lieutenant who has been home since the battle of Newbern where he was wounded. I supose you have heard of the death of Joe Grummond.

I have talked with a number of rebel prisoners lately and the more inteligent of them say that the late raid into Md. was a desperate thing, but they had to do something as they were in such a bad fix in Virginia that the war will soon have to be brought to a close. Well Mother I am about tired of writing so I will stop. I will write again soon if I have a chance I would like to see you all very much and mabe I will get a chance to come home before a great while. Good bye Mother Much love to Mattie, the Baby and all the rest. G. W. Whitman

Wednesday Sept 24th I have not had a chance to send this letter since it was written but I hear, a mail will leave here to day so I open this to let you know that we are still here and that everything is quiet G. W. W.

Near Antietam Md. Sept 30th 1862

Dear Mother

We are still laying quietly at the place from which I dated my last letter. I thought when I wrote you last which was 5 or 6 days since that we should cross over into Virginia before now, but as we are comfortably situated, I think very likely we will remain here for some time. Everything now is quiet and it is quite a releif to be out of the sound of canon after hearing it almost daily, and sometimes nightly, for two or three weeks. I think the late rebel movement into Maryland has been a very unfortunate one for them, as they did not meet with anything like the encouragement from the Marylanders that they expected, and I believe that after the battle of Bull Run they firmly expected to invade Pennsylvania if not capture Washington and Baltimore, and now to be badly beaten twice, and driven back with such terrible loss, must be very discouraging and had it not been for bad management, cowardice or treachery at Harpers Fery, I believe we could have bagged the most of their army.

We are now about 8 miles from Harpers Fery and are in the midst of Mountains, from which the view is very fine indeed. We have enough to eat and plenty of good cool spring water. We have been provided with shelter tents, which are made of two peices of light canvas about 6 ft square each which button togather in the centre and make one tent to accomodate two men, they are very good on account of the heavy dews we have here, and for a shade, but as the two ends are open they are not much use in a storm. When we move the occupants of a tent each take half roll it and tie it on their backs so we always have our houses with us and can make ourselves at home wherever we stop.

Mother the last letter I received from home is dated

Sept 8th and I hope if you have not writen you will write as soon as you get this. The captain of our company has gone home on a twenty days furlough. I believe he intends to stop a few days in New York at the Astor House. Tryon our 1st Lieut that was in New York recruiting has returned, he has a position as Aide on General Ferrero's Staff. So that I am in command of the company. A Corporal from our company, started for New York, on recruiting service this morning. I told him if he had a chance to call on you and send me word how you all are. His name is John Cambot and he was sent to report to Major Le Gendre at his office on Broadway, where he can be found.

I expect there will shortly be some promotions made in the regt and I think I stand a good chance to be made a 1st Lieut. I think, after Cap gets back if everything remains quiet I shall try for a furlough to come home for a few days and see you all. I have stuck pretty close to buisness since I have been sogering, and the regt never went on a march or into a fight without my being on hand. (I see by the papers that Uncle Abe has issued a proclamation declaring the slaves free in all the States that are in rebellion on the first of next Jan. I dont know what effect it is going to have on the war but one thing is certain, he has got to lick the south before he can free the niggers,) and unless he drives ahead and convinces the south, before the first of January, that we are bound to lick them, and it would be better for them, to behave themselvs and keep their slaves, than to get licked and lose them, I dont think the proclamation will do much good.

Mother I have three months pay due me to day so dont deprive yourself of anything you need.

Direct my letters Sturgis Division, Ferreros Brigade 9th Army Corps I often think that I can imagine just what you

are all doing at home and ile bet now, that Mother is makeing pies.   I think Mat is putting up shirt bosoms like the
deuce so as to get through before dinner   I guess Sis is down
stairs helping Mother mix the dough, Walt is up stairs
writing, Jeff is down town at the office, Jess is pealing
Potatoes for dinner, and Tobias[1] has gone down cellar for a
scuttle of coal, Bunkum I guess is around somewhere looking for a good chance to go sogering.

Well Mother take good care of yourself and dont get
exciteded.

Much love to all
G. W. Whitman

I think I shall write to Boss Rac in a day or two

Camp near Falmouth
Thursday night Jan 22d/63

Dear Mother.

I have just written to Walt, and although it is
pretty late, I must write you a few lines while my hand
is in, to let you know that I am well and hearty.   We have
had a very heavy storm here for the last 48 hours, rain-
ing and blowing like great guns, but it appears to be
about played out now.   There has been a movement on foot
here for the last Three days but I dont think it will amount
to anything as I am afraid the storm has interfeered with
the movement and spoiled Burnsides plans.   The Army commenced to move from here early on Tuesday morning last,
going somewhere up the river, but I dont know how far.   I
believe our Army Corps are the only troops left here, (but
you musent say anything about it Mother or the rebs might
hear of it and come over here and eat us all up) my oppinion
is, that it was intended to throw a heavy force accross the

---

[1] "Tobias" probably was a nickname for Edward Whitman.

river, somewhere above here, and let them come down and attack Fredericksburg in the rear or on the flank while we occupied their attention in front, with our Batteries on this side of the river, but whatever the plan was, I believe it had to be given up, on account of the storm, or it would have been commenced before now.

I forget whether I have written home, since I got the letter from Jeff, with the money, or not, anyhow the money came all right. I got a letter from Walt. to night with a lot of postage stamps and envelopes allready directed some to you Mammy, and some to Jeff. Walt says he has a prospect of getting a pretty good berth in Washington. Heyde wrote me a letter a few days ago saying that Hannah was quite sick, and I immediately wrote to Walt to either go on there and bring her home, or make some arangement to have her come on at once. and in his letter to night Walt says he is confident she is either home or on her way there. I hope she is not as sick as Heyde makes it apear. but we would all feel a great deal better satisfied if she was home. Mother tell her to write to me as soon as she gets home.

Well Mother how are you all getting along, Mattie and Sis I hope are well, somehow or annother I cant help thinking of Sis as she was when I came away I cant seem to make out how big she must be by this time, and I think if you would write me, how many pancakes she can eat I could tell about how much she has grown since I came away.

Well Mother it is getting chilly sitting here in my tent as the fire has gone out, so I must bid you.

good night

dear Mother

G. W. Whitman

Heusonville [Hustonville] Ky. May 29th/63

Dear Mother.

My last letter home, was written from Lancaster and dated somewhere about the 16th or 18th of May. Since then we have been on the move again as you see by the heading of this. We left Lancaster on the morning of the 23d, marched about 11 miles and bivouaced at a place called Crab Orchard, and stopped untill the morning of the 25th when we came on about 10 miles further and bivouaced near the Villiage of Stamford. Next morning we started on again and after a march of 10 miles more we arrived and pitched our camp at this place. We have a first rate camping ground, in a grove just outside the town, and are takeing things very comfortable. Our Regt. is the only troops here, the rest of our Brigade being at Stamford. Of course we dont know how long we shall stay here, or which way we will move next. We do picket duty on the roads, about the country here, and our chief business is, to look out for rebel Cavelry raids, as they have been in the habit of dashing through these small country towns, stealing horses and Cattle and everything else they wanted. We had quite an excitement the first night after our arrival here. We put up our tents, on the afternoon of our arrival, and I was promising myself a good nights sleep (as we were all pretty tired after our march, and the work of pitching camp) but about 9 O clock at night, we were ordered to strike tents immediately, so we had to turn out and take down and load tents, pack trunks, and get ready for a move, which we did at short notice. As soon as the things, were all loaded, I enquired around to try and find out what the fuss was all about, and when I did find out I felt mad enough I can tell you. It seems that somebody had passed our pickets, who said he was carrying dispatches, to somebody, who was stationed somewhere, and that the dispatches were from General Carter, and that the rebs had crossed the Cumberland River, and were in strong force, at a place called Liberty about 10 miles from here, and were comeing on this way. As soon as I heard the yarn I said it was a devilish foolish hoax, as I was satisfied that the enemy could never get as far in the state, as Liberty, without our hearing of it, and I dident like the idea of loseing my nights sleep for nothing. The wagon train started off towards the rest of our Brigade, and we fell in and marched about ½ a mile, and halted and stayed in the road all night. Next morning we came back here, and encamped again.

Mother I have not heard from you in quite a long time. I had a letter from Walt a few days ago, he said that all at home, was going on the same as usual. Andrew he thought would go to Newbern with Cornell, Mary I hear has been down and paid you a visit, Walt says, probaly, Mary will go on to Burlington for Hannah, and bring her home. Mother, how are you getting along, does the rheumatism bother you much now. Mattie, and Sis, Walt says are first rate. Jess, and Ed. I suppose can take their rations regular. Jeff wrote to me three or four weeks ago, he says that as long as I dont hear from home I may know that all is right. That wont do Jeff. its a pretty good way to get off, but I dont see it.

The news from Grant, down at Vicksburg is very encouraging, I only hope it wont turn out like the news of the capture of Richmond. If it should turn out, that Vicksburg is certain to fall into our hands in this campain it will be a heavy blow to the rebs.

I have just got Jeffs letter of the 22d. Mother I am very sory to hear that you are again troubled with rheumatism. I hope you wont attempt to work untill you get well. how about the vapor baths do you take them now, but

I hope you are better by this time. Andrew to Jeff says is quite bad   I hope he will take good care of himself, and soon get well, All the rest I am glad to hear are getting along first rate and are in good health, I hope, as Han (according to Heydes letter) has commenced to get well she will soon be able to come home. Take good care of yourself dear Mother, and let me hear from you often.

Much love to Mattie, and Sis, and all the rest,
Geo. W. Whitman

Camp of 51st Regt N. Y. Vols.
Near Milldale Miss. July 23d/63

Dear Mother

I take the first oppertunity I have had in some time to let you know that I am well and hearty. I fear Mother that you have been somewhat worried about not hearing from me in so long, but we have been so situated that there was no chance to send letters away, even if we had a chance to write them. I got a letter from Walt, a few days ago, dated July 5th, he tells me you have another Sissy at your house, I only hope she is as smart and bright as Sissy No One.

We returned to camp this morning after about as hard a campaign of 19 days as I want to see. We are now back in the same camp we occupied before the fall of Vicksburg, this is the position where we expected to whip Johnson, if he had attempted to come to the relief of Pemberton. We are between the Yazoo and Black rivers and about 7 miles directly in the rear of Vicksburg. (Our whole corps were encamped around here, before the surrender of Vicksburg, and we had dug miles of rifle pitts, and would have had a big thing on Johnson, if we could have got him to come here and give us a fight. Vicksburg you reccolect surrendered on the morning of July 4th, and on the afternoon of the same day, we started off to find Johnson, as it was certain he would not come here to us. After a march of about 10 miles, our advance came up to the enemys pickets, who were posted on the opposite side of the Big Black river, (a deep creek about 100 feet wide) as soon as we came in sight the rebel pickets skeedadled, and we had to stop and wait, (nearly two days) untill a bridge was built, before we could cross. As soon as the bridge was ready we pushed on after the rebs, the dust laying in the road like flour, 4 or 5 inches thick, and the weather terrible hot, quite a number of the men fell down in the ranks, from the effects of the sun, and there was considerable suffering from the scarscity of water and we were forced to drink, from any little pond that could be found by the way no matter how bad the water was. Grub to was mighty scarce, and green corn was the chief article of food.

The enemy did not pretend to make a stand, untill they got behind their entrenchments at Jackson, this City you know is the Capitol of the state and is built on the bank of the Pearl river, their earthworks started from the river above the town and ran along the outskirts untill they struck the river again just below the city, makeing a line of about 3 miles in length.. The enemy were supposed to be from 25 to 30,000 strong and on the afternoon of July Tenth we drove their skirmishers, inside of their entrenchments, and we threw forward a heavy line of skirmishers, reaching nearly the whole length of the enemys line, and within easy rifle range of the enemys works. Each Brigade had a certain part of the line, and the regts, releived each other every 24 hours that is, the ones that were up to the front one day, were moved back a short distance, the next, and held in reserve, but had to be ready, at any moment to fall in, and sometimes when we heard heavy fireing, we had to fall in two or three times during the night. It seemed very curious fighting to me, and very different from what we had been used to. There was no general engagement but during the day, and sometimes during the night, quite a brisk fire was kept by sharpshooters on each side, Each party kept themselvs concealed as much as possible, the enemy behind their earthworks, and our side behind trees, and by laying flat on the ground and the moment anyone showed themselvs there was two or three rifles pointed at them. I expected Gen. Sherman (who I believe had command on our side) intended to skirmish with them, and keep them buisy on this side of the river, while someone crossed the river, and made an attack on the rear, which of course would have cutt off their retreat, but for some probably good reason (that I know nothing about) nothing of the kind was attempted, as far as I can hear. The skirmish was kept up untill about daylight on the morning of the 17th when a white flag was run up, by some citazens on one of the rebel works and we soon found that the whole rebel force had skedaddled during the night, and we went in and occupied the place. Our Brigade was the first troops inside the town, and the 51st was the second Regt. We found the place very much damaged by our Artillery, and nearly deserted by the inhabitants, what few citazens we found had dug holes or burrows in the ground and there they had staid while the fighting was going on. The loss on our side, has been very light indeed and our regt. only had one man wounded, we took three or four hundred prisoners, and quite a large number of rifles and considerable ammunition fell into our hands. (Soon after we entered the town the western troops began to come in, and they ransacked and plundered the town completely. The western armies burn and destroy every thing they come across and the same number of men, marching through the country, will do three times the damage of the army of the Potomac. Sometimes on the march, I have known them to break and destroy, the most costly furniture such as Pianos and Sofas, and I have seen the roads strewn with the most splendid bound books, that would be taken from the libraries, carried a little distance and thrown away.) The planters had generaly left their houses, (when they found the yanks were comeing,) leaving darkies in charge, and the troops would often burn the houses, and the darkies would run away, and follow the sogers. We traveled through thousands of acres of corn, and sometimes 4 or 5,000 men with two or three hundred horses and mules would bivouac in a corn field. When we left here we only took the clothes we had on leaving our trunks here in camp, and two or three times I have went to a pond and took off my clothes and washed them myself, and two or three times I have been completely soaked with the rain, and laid down at night on the ground, (after drinking a cup of coffe and eating a cracker) and slept soundly all night, and got up at 4 O clock next morning feeling first rate, and I am now as well as ever I was in my life. We dont know how long we will stay here, or which way we will move next, but the general impression is, that we will start back for Kentucky in the course of a few days, so I think very likely the next letter you have from me will be from Kentuck. You sent me a letter that you had received from Hannah. Poor Hann, O how I should like to see her, I was very glad to hear from her, but very, very sory to hear that she was recovering from her sickness so slowly. I was expecting to hear that she, was about comeing home I feel certain if she was only well enough to come home, that she would soon be well. Mother, you must urge her to come on just as soon as she is well enough to stand the journey.

I have seen a New York Herald, as late as July 9th it seems, that the Army of the Potomac, has at last done something pretty nice, the paper speaks as though the capture of Lee's Army was certain, but we have had him in a tight spot so often before that I cant help thinking that he will manage some way to get off. Walt seems to be getting along very well there in Washington. Andrew he says did not go to Newbern. I am glad to hear that he is getting better of his throat disease. I hope Mother, when we get back to Kentucky that I shall hear from you again often. Mattie and the baby, Walt says are getting along finely. Mother I hope you are well, you must take things easy this hot weather. Tell Jeff to write to me often and let me know how things are getting along at home and Mother, you must write yourself as often as you can get a chance.

I see by Walts letter that you have received the 200 dollars that I sent you at last pay.

Good bye Dear Mother Kind regards to all.
Geo. W. Whitman

Camp Nelson Ky. Oct. 16th/63

Dear Mother,

What can be the reason that some of you dont write to me. I have been expecting every day, for the last two weeks to get a letter from home, but every day I have been disapointed

I had a letter from Walt, dated Sept. 28th he said that Andrew was considerable better and was Doctoring with a celabrated Italian Doctor in Court St. I dont have much faith in them new fangled foreign Doctors, but if Andrew is realy so much better, it is good encouragement to keep on and give him a fair trial. All the rest at home Walt. says, are as well as usual. Mother I hope you are takeing things easy and comfortable, and above all I hope that you dont wory, and work, as much as you used to. Matty and the babies I hear are first rate.

Whenever you hear from Hannah, you must let me know how she is getting along, and if she is comeing home soon.

Walt says that you received the money all right, I suppose he means the last I sent you ($187.00) about Sept. 9th. Everything here with me is just the same as when I last wrote you (two or three weeks ago, did you get it) our Regt. you know is temporarily detatched from the Brigade and stationed at this Post, there is a great quantity of Quatermaster, and Commissary Stores collected here, which we have to guard

There is scarsely any sickness in the Regt. now, as our camp is very dry and healthy and is kept perfectly clean. I dont hear any talk of our leaving here, so I think the chances are that we will stay here some time. I am just as comfortable here as can be, I have first rate grub, a good stove, plenty of wood, and everything nice. Does Jeff ever see Capt. Sims or Lieut. Mc Ready about Brooklyn, I wonder what their chances are for getting conscripts. it seem the draft was almost a failure, what is going to be done now, will there be another draft, or will they fall back on the old volunteer plan, with big bounties, I am rather in favor of the draft, I should very much like to see that party of suckers, that stay at home and oppose the Government, forced to come out here and take a rifle, for I think just the meanest rebels that ever lived, are those that stay at home and oppose the draft, and blow about the violation of the Constitution, the liberties of the People, and all that sort of thing, and if it was possible to make them come out here, and let the old troops drive them into the next fight, (with Seymour and the Woods[1] in the front rank) I think it would be a fine thing, and I am certain that the sooner something is done to stop the mouths of that class of cowardly traitors, the sooner the war will be brought to a close.

The election last Tuesday in Ohio was a grand victory for our side, dont you Yorkers feel a little ashamed about your election last Fall, when you see how other states treat such chaps as Seymoure & Vallandigham.[2]

Jeff, how is it that you never write to a fellow now a days, ime a good mind to get mad at all of you. Mattie whats the news at your house, have you got lots of good things put away for the winter I make lots of reckoning, of good dinners with you, if I come home this winter.

Mother dont neglect to write as soon as you get this, and let me know all the particulars of your affairs. I am very anxious to hear from Andrew. I think I shall write to Walt to night or tomorrow Direct your letters to me at Camp Nelson Ky 51st Regt N. Y. V. but dont put on the Brigade, Division, or Corps, as I think perhaps the reason of my not hearing from you is, that you have directed, to the Corps, and the letters have gone on to the front, the rest of the 9th Corps being somewhere about Knoxville Tenn.

Good bye all, for the present.

Geo. W. Whitman

Camp Pittman near London Ky. Dec. 9th/63

Dear Mother

I have just received a letter from Jeff. of Dec. 3d bringing the sorrowful news of the death of Brother An-

---

[1] Horatio Seymour, opponent of the draft and often called a "Copperhead," was in 1862 elected Governor of New York. Fernando Wood and his brother Benjamin were "Peace Democrats" who opposed the draft.

[2] Clement L. Vallandigham, a "Peace Democrat" or "Copperhead," was defeated in the election for Governor of Ohio in 1863.

drew. I was somewhat prepared for the worst, by Walts letter of Dec. 1st but I still had strong hopes, that he would recover, and until I received Walts letter, I had no idea that Andrew was in any immediate danger.

Mother I am very glad to hear that Mary has been down to see you, and was with poor Andrew during his last hours, and am very sory that Walt did not stay with you a few days longer. Jeff speaks of my trying for a leave of absence but I hardly think it would be of any use at present, besides I dont know that I could do any good by comeing home, although I am very anxious to see you all.

Mother I wish you or Jeff would write me a long letter giving the particulars about Andrews family and what Nancy proposes to do. Was Andrew burried at Cyprus Hill Cemetry. I would advise buying a plott of ground there if you have not done so already.

Mother I do hope that you will bear up with your troubles, and not make yourself sick by worrying. Walt wrote me that Matty and all the rest of you were doing everything in the world that could be done for Andrew and it is some consolation to know that he died surrounded by friends and relatives, who were anxious to make his last hours as comfortable as possible, while so many are dying (out here) with no one about them who seems to take the least interest in them. I yesterday received a letter from Walt, enclosing one from Hannah dated Nov 21st, Hannah seems to be much better now than when I last heard from her, and I hope to hear soon, of her coming home to pay you a long visit.

Mother you see by this that we have moved from Crab Orchard, we came on here last week, this place is 38 miles from Crab Orchard, in the direction of Cumberland Gap. How long we will remain here, of course we dont know, but there is strong talk of our being ordered home to re-organize and as nearly all of our men are anxious to re-enlist in the veteran Corps, I think that the chances are that we will be ordered home before many weeks. I sent you $150,00 by Addams Express a few days ago, I was on to Lexington Ky. to Express the money for the men, and sent it from there, Mother dont be the least backward in useing the money for anything you want, and I know, you will do all, that is required for Andrews Family I dont feel like writing more to night, so good night dear Mother. Give my love to all

G. W. Whitman

I am in as good health as ever I was in my life

Camp near Annapolis Md
April 14th 1864

Dear Mother,

We were paid this afternoon for the Month of Febru-ary, and I enclose you $50.00 and am sorry that I cant send you more, but Mother if you need more before I get my next pay (which is due the last of this Month) you must certainly draw it from the Bank, as I send it to you for you to use it just when you want it.

Mother I received your letter (of April 6th) a few days ago. I had felt quite alarmed about you—as Walt wrote me that you had a very bad cough, and I know how any thing of that kind affects and hangs on to you. I am quite sure Mother that you are not half carefull enough of yourself, and if you would only hire someone to come and work for you two or three days every week, and let them do all the scrubing and cleaning, I am sure you would not be trobled so much with colds and lameness, You needent say you cant afford it Mammy, for I will guarentee to send you money enough to keep the Institution running (without your working the way you always have) and Mammy dont you be backward in useing it. One thing is certain Mammy you must surely contrive to take more care of yourself, and in your next letter I shall expect to hear that you have made some arrangement that will enable you to sit down and take your ease whenever you feel like it. Ime in right down earnest Mammy, and if you will only do as I advise I shall be a great deal better satisfied.

I know you think that no one can do your work like yourself. (Mammy I wonder what the duece you would do if you was unfortunate enough to be rich) but you cant expect to work now as you did Twenty or Thirty years ago, so you have just got to take things easy and get some one else to do the hard work or let it go undone.

Matty and the little gals you say are well, poor little Sis I felt quite worried about her after I went away, You know she was pretty bad with the croupe a night or two before I left home. Hattie can knock around and hold her own almost anywhere, does she go in and tease aunty Brown's parrot now a days.

So Mother you are all going to stay in Portland Ave another year, well I dont suppose you could do better, for the same rent, although if the house was smaller or the Rent rather so that you and Mattie could take the whole of it it would be much better.

I received a letter from Walt dated April 9th he seems to be getting along very well and says he thinks of publishing a small book this Spring.[1] I should like very much to hear from Hannah and whenever you hear from her, Mother you must not fail to let me know. I am first rate and am getting along tip top, when I last wrote you I believe we were in

---

[1] *Drum-Taps*, which did not appear, however, until 1865.

barracks. We are now encamped about 2½ miles from the Villiage and we have everything as nice and comfortable as you please, we have been pretty short of cash along back but as we are paid now, we can go it with a rush. Hunt the man that I told you was going Sutler for the Regt and intended to board the Officers, did not go with us to Tennessee, but he is here now and expects to have the institution running in the course of a day or two. I think it will save us a good deal of trouble, and be much better than liveing as we have been. I have a nice wall tent all alone to myself and if I have some one to look out for my grub, I shall be all hunk. I dont see any signs of our leaving here yet awhile, Troops arrive here almost every day and go into Camp. We have only had some 60 or 70 recruits as yet, but we hear there are some 200 in New York for us.

Generals Grant, and Burnside, paid us a visit yesterday. There was no grand Review as is generaly the case, but the Regiments just fell in line and Grant rode along and looked at them and then went on about his business. There are all sorts of speculation about the destination of our Expedition but the general opinion is that we are to go to North Carolina for an advance into Virginia by way of Goldsborough while the Potomac Army makes another push for Richmond by the front door, but I am rather inclined to think that we are intended as a kind of reserve, to send where we are most needed.

Mother I believe I mentioned in my last letter about your haveing some of my pictures taken and sent on to me by mail as I have promised several of the Officers to give them one. And about the boots if no one is wearing them if Jeff would wrap them up and send them by Express and send me the receipt by mail, they would be good for stormy weather, but if any one is wearing them its of no consequence. Good bye for the present. Dear Mother, give my love to all and let me hear from you often. Direct Capt G. W. W. Co K 51 Regt N. Y. Vols Annapolis Md

> About Two miles from Peters-
> burg Va. June 18th/64

Dear Mother.

I got a letter from Walt yesterday (dated June 11th) enclosing one from you of June 8th and you dont know how glad I was to hear that you are all well. It has been some time Mother, since I have had a chance to write to you, and I have felt quite bad for fear that you would frett and worry about not hearing from me, and I have often thought, I would give almost anything to let you know that I was all right. The last time I wrote you, I believe we were some-where near Coal Harbor (although I dont think I knew the name of the place when I wrote) and since then we have been kept pretty buissy building rifle pitts, cutting roads and throwing up earthworks &c (I believe I told you in my last letter that our Regt had been detached from the Brigade and was doing duty as an Engineer Regt) we like the change first rate as we are not expected to take much part in the fighting, but as our folks drive the enemy, or take a new position we go to work and fortify it.

The most of our work has to be done at night, and we often surprise the enemy in the morning, with works that we have made during the night within 4 or 500 yards of their line of battle. About half of our Regt. are detailed as Head Quarter Guard for Genl Burnside and are on duty at the Generals quarters, so you see Mother we are having pretty good times, and I rather think the old 51st have struck a streak of luck at last. Sometimes we are rather short of grub, and sometimes pretty well played out with hard work, but as long as we are gaining ground, I dont grumble at hard work or short rations.

We had quite a lively little time a few days before we left Coal Harbor. Capt Sims and myself (I have been acting Major for the last Month) took the Regt out on the skirmish line one afternoon to build rifle pitts, and as we were in plain sight of the rebel skirmishers we were considerably puzzled how to work without exposing our men to much, for as soon as the men began to dig the rebs commenced to blaze away at them, and we were likely to loose quite a number of men, so I proposed a new plan I got a lot of empty cracker boxes and stationed the men about 10 ft apart, gave each man a box, and made him crawl out on the line lay down behind the box fill it with earth, and then I took each one annother box so that in a very few minutes the men had first rate protection and could work without much danger, and everything was going on finely when just as I had sett down to take a cup of Coffe, I heard the rebs give a yell as they charged down our front. Our boys dropped their spades and seized their rifles that were stacked near at hand and in a few minutes we cleared our front entirely of the enemy, but a regt. that was working on our right gave way and allowed the rebs to come round our right flank, and as I saw there was no way for us to prevent the enemy getting around in the rear of us and takeing us all prisoners I gave the order to fall back to the next line of breastworks where our troops lay in line of battle, I did not much like the idea of being drove off and before I left the rebs were some 100 feet in the rear of our line, but I knew a way down through a ravine, that I could get out all right. We lost one man killed 4 or 5 wounded and some 6 or 7 taken prisoners, and I hear the Regt. gets considerable credit at Head Quarters for the way it behaved.

We arrived here day before yesterday and found the fight going on and it has been kept up ever since (sometimes very sharp and then again it dies away) ever since we arrived here. So far the fighting along the front of our Corps has been altogather in our favor and we have been steadily driving the rebs ever since we came here, and now as I write there is a very savage fight going on in our front, and I think by the fireing that our boys are pushing the enemy back and unless the rebs can make a firmer stand than they have made here yet it will not be long before the long covetted City of Petersburg will be in our possession I notice by the papers that our Corps is very little spoken of, but for all that they have done some splendid fighting, although we seem to be, rather outsiders here in the Army of the Potomac, and Genl Burnside is one of these kind of men that does the work they give him to doo and finds no fault and I am sure I dont object to the noble Potomac Army's getting their full share of praise.

Our Corps met with quite a serious loss yesterday in the death of the Cheif Engineer of the Corps Major Morton. Our Division (the 2d) had just carried a very formidable line of rebel works and Major Morton had just gone up on the line to lay out some work for our Regt. to do as soon as it got dark, when he was hitt in the side with a rifle ball and died almost instantly.

He was a good friend to our Regt and is very much regretted by the whole Corps. Last night I took the Regt up on the line and worked all night. We were in a large open plain, our Batteries were just behind us and the rebel Batteries were just in front of us, and Three or four times during the night the Batteries opened on each other and kept up a pretty sharp fire for 10 or 15 minutes and then they would quiet down again. It was splendid where we was, both parties fired over our heads, but so high that we were in no danger, and we could watch the shells bursting in front and rear of us, and down to the right and left, we could plainly see both lines of skirmishers blazing away at each other, and could eaisily tell by the direction of the flame as it left the rifles which was our line and which the rebs.

Well Mother I hope you wont keep yourself in a frett this hot weather but just keep as cool as possible. I am very anxious to see you all, but if I cannot see you the next best thing is to hear from you often and whenever you hear from Hannah, dont fail to send me the letter. Good bye Mother for the present   Much love to all.

G. W. Whitman

In front of Petersburg Va
10 O clock Tuesday night Aug 9th/64

Dear Mother.

I have just come in from the front, where we have been on picket for the last 48 hours, and as everything is quiet, and I dont care to turn in just yet, I will do as I promised the last time I wrote, (I see by Walts letter of Aug. 4th that you got mine all right,) and tell you something about our fight here on the 30th of last Month.

Well Mother, to begin at the begining, you must know that for 4 or 5 weeks before the great blow up came off, one of the Regts. of our Brigade (the 48th Penn.) had been at work digging a mine, starting about 100 feet in rear of the line that our Regt. occupies when on picket, and running under a rebel fort, just to the left and front of us, and about 175 yards from where the mine started. This was quite a great undertaking and as I understand, pronounced by the regular Engineers of the Potomac Army as not at all likely to suceed, but the Regt. that had the work in charge are nearly all Coal Miners from Penn. and their Lieut. Col. (Pleasants) was a mining Engineer at home, so they just kept on at their work, and on the 29th of last month, the thing was all charged and ready to touch off. On the Evening of the 29th (our Regt being on picket at the time) we were notified to be ready to leave the rifle pitts at a moments notice, and somewhere about 4 O clock on the morning of the 30th we were ordered to leave a small force in the pitts to keep up the usual amount of fireing (so that the enemy wouldent suspect anything) and to fall back about a quarter of a mile with the rest of the Regt. and wait for orders.

After going back as we were ordered, we waited for an hour, and had made up our minds that the thing was a failure (as the fuse had been lighted before we left the pitts and it was expected to take about 25 minutes to burn to the magazines) when we felt the earth tremble under our feet, and immidately a vast column of earth was thrown up in the air very much resembling (in shape) a hugh water spout, and as we hear since burying in its fall several guns and quite a number of Rebs. The Artillerymen all along our line were standing by their guns ready to fire, and the very second the explosion took place the fire from nearly a hundred peices of Artillery opened along our line, and take it all togather I think it was the most exciting sight I ever saw.

From what I have since learned, I think the programe was something like this. I think it was intended the instant the Fort was blown up, for the First Division of our Corps (who were formed close up to the front) to charge through the First line of the enemy, and push on to the second, which it was expected during the panic and surprise of the enemy they could easily take and hold. Our Division the 2d was then to charge on the right, and the Third on the left, while the Fourth Division (the Darkies) were to be thrown forward, passing through the First Division, and advancing on to Petersburg, the Fourth Division to be followed and suported by parts of the 5th 10th & 18th corps, who were massed just inside our lines. The plan I think was a good one and as yet, I cant see why, with proper management it couldent have been carried out, but it seems the First Division that should have been moved forward on the instant, did not (for some reason or another) advance for some time after the explosion, and then only as far as the enemys 1st line. About half an hour after the fight commenced our Division was brought up to the front and our Regt and the 2d N. Y. of our Brigade was put in our old rifle pitts, while the rest of the Division was sent on to where the rebel Fort had been.

It seems that after the fort was blown up it still formed a sort of breastwork, as the earth thrown from the centre made quite a bank around the sides, and in this excavation and in the traverses or pitts surounding the fort our men crowded for protection from the rebel Artillery and the talk is that the men could not be got forward to the second line, but my own opinion is that if some of the men with stars on their shoulders, had led the way the men wouldent have been backward in following them. As it was our Division being sent there only made matters worse, for almost every place that would afford any protection was crowded already, and so much time had been lost, that the rebs had massed a heavy force on their second line, and it would have been pretty hard work to cary it by assault. Our Division made one or two feeble attempts but were driven back each time. It must have been horrible lying in that crowded place, as there was quite a large number of dead and wounded among them, and several peices of Artillery were throwing shot and shell in there constantly. The day was very hot indeed, and they could not get a drop of water, and many of the men were completely exhausted. In order to get back to our lines, they would have had to cross an open field about one hundred yards wide, which was completely swept by the enemy's Artillery and Infantry, some few of them tried it but the most of those that made the attempt were either killed or wounded.

About 9 O clock the order was given for our Regt. to charge the rifle pitts in front of us. Major Wright was in command of the Regt. Capt Sims was acting Lieut Col. and had charge of the right wing, and I was acting Major and had charge of the left. As soon as the order was given to charge, I jumped up on the breastworks and sung out for the men to follow me, and the way they tumbled over them breastworks wasent slow. Poor Cap Sims led the right wing in fine style, and just before we reached their works the Johnies skedaddled. Our orders were to take the works and hold them, but after we had held them for about two hours, the rebs massed a heavy force, in a ravine just in front of us, but out of our sight, and came down on us like a whirlwind, and we were forced to fall back to our old line of works. I tried my best, to keep the men from falling back, but Capt. Sims was killed just at this time so it was no use trying to rally the men untill they got behind their old works. The rebel charge was one of the boldest and most desperate things I ever saw, but if our men had staid there and fought as they ought, we could have inflicted a heavy loss on the enemy, before they could have driven us away from there. The rebs did not attempt to follow us beyond their works but they kept up a sharp fire on us from behind their breastworks, but as far as our losses are concerned our Regt got off very lucky, I think about 40 killed and wounded.

Our troops in the fort held out till long after we were driven back, and several times the rebs charged right up to the bank, and some of them jumped over among our men, and went at it hand to hand, and before our men surrendered quite a good deal of fighting was done with the bayonet alone, but finaly they saw there was no help for them, and they were forced to surrender, and so the fight ended each side holding the same ground as at the commencment. One of the worst things of the whole affair was, that quite a number of our wounded lay between the rebel lines and ours, and there the poor creatures had to lay in the sun, untill the afternoon of the next day, when the rebs allowed us to send out a flag of truce to give them water, but they wouldent allow any of them to be removed untill the second day after the fight when a ceecession of hostilities was agreed to for three or four hours, when what few were alive were brought off and the dead were burried.

During the ceecession of hostilities some of our boys went out and brought in the boddy of Capt. Sims and it is now on the way to Brooklyn.

Well Mother I think that is talk enough about fighting for this time. Things with us are going the same as ever, we have not been paid yet, but we expect the paymaster in the course of a day or two. Mother I should like very much to have you send me a dozen of my pictures (those you sent to me at Annapolis you know I never received) as I have promised them to several Officers, and they keep bothering me about them all the while, I should like very much also for Walt. to send me one of his new books as soon as it is published.[1]

Jeff asked me in a letter a short time ago, if there was

---

[1] The "new book" was *Drum-Taps*, which did not appear until 1865. The request for a copy disproves the contention sometimes made that George Whitman was wholly indifferent to his brother's poetry.

any chance for a fellow (in case he was drafted) to get a substitute from the men of our who are discharged at the expiration of their term of service.   None of the men who have been through this Campaign, will listen to Re-enlisting at present   they all think they have had sogering enough and its no use talking to them untill they have been home a month or two, then probaly a good many of them will change their minds.

Mother dont neglect to let me know whenever you hear from Hannah.   I commenced this letter last night (the 9th) but soon got sleepy and turned in, and I now begin to fell the same way so I will wind up and go to bed.

Give my love to Mattie and all.

Good night.

G. W. Whitman

when you sent the pictures Mother please send them by Mail

About 5 miles from Petersburg Va near
Weldon Rail Road August 30th 1864

Dear Mother.

Your letter and Walts containing the pictures came all right, and yesterday I received another from Walt, saying that you had received the money.

We have moved 4 or 5 miles since I wrote you last.   We came here on the 19th and expected to have a right smart fight, but so far, we have been very agreeably disapointed, as our Division has not been engaged to any extent.   The first night we came here I was ordered (as I was in command of the Regt) to deploy the Regt. as skirmishers and advance through a peice of woods where the enemy had been in considerable force a few hours previous, I thought we were in for a fight sure, but upon advancing and taking the position, as ordered, we found the enemy had fell back, and next morning we advanced ½ a mile further to this place and here we have remained since.

We have a splendid position here, and are very strongly entrenched, have plenty of shade, plenty to eat, plenty of good water, and are very comfortable.

I think we have got this Rail Road all right, although the enemy may make another effort to drive us away, but I dont believe they will meet with any better success than they have in the three attempts they have made already, they have been pretty severely punished each time and may not think it worth while to try it again but if they are not satisfied let them keep on trying, we are prepared for them.

I am in command of the Regt. as Major Wright is away somewhere sick. I send you Maj. Wrights Official report, of the fight on the 30th of July.[1]

I am very glad to hear that Jeff is clear of the draft, on the 5th of next month, although $400 seems like a pretty large sum to pay for a substitute.

Walt says he is getting all right again,—when his book is published I would him, to send me a coppy. Mattie and the children I hear are well as usual.

Mother I hope you take thing easy and dont worry, and keep a bright look out for that little place in the country. When I get the New York papers I almost always look over the Farms for sale to see if there is anything offered that will suit us.

Walt has asked several times if Williams (who was with

---

[1] The report of Captain John G. Wright, dated Aug. 8, 1864, includes the following reference to George Whitman: "The Command of the Regiment then devolved upon Captain George W. Whitman the next Senior Officer. I am happy to say he discharged the duties of the responsible position to my entire satisfaction, and it affords me great pleasure to speak of the gallant manner in which he has sustained himself during this entire campaign" (MS in Trent Collection).

Fred Mc Cready) was captured when the ambulance train was attacted. Williams is here with his Company he says when the guerillas ordered the train to halt, he jumped over the fence and escaped.

    Kind regards to all

George W. Whitman

Danville Va. October 23d 1864

Dear Mother. I wrote you a line from Libby Prison a few days after I was taken prisoner, but think it doubtfull if you received it. I was taken, (along with almost our entire Regt. both Officers and men) on the 30th day of September, near the Weldon Rail Road, but am proud to think that we stood and fought untill we were entirely surrounded, Major Wright, Lieuts Pooley, Sims, and 9 other Officers of our Regt, are here, Capt Walton and Lieut Butler was wounded, but I dont know how badly, I am verry well indeed, and in tip top spirits, am tough as a mule, and about as ugly, and can eat any amount of corn bread, so you see, *dear Mother* that I am all right, and my greatest trouble is that you will worry about me, but I beg of you not to frett, as I get along first rate. Please write to Lieut. Babcock Co F of our Regt. and tell him to send my things home by Express. Much love to all.

G. W. Whitman

Officers Hospital Annapolis Md.
Feb. 24th 1865

Dear Mother.

    I arrived here yesterday from the Hotel De Libby and if ever a poor devil was glad to get in a Christian Country it was me.

    I am perfectly well Mother although I am in the

Hospital Buildings, and am not under Medical treatment. The reason that I am quartered here is that the Hotels and Boarding Houses in town are cramed full, I stay here for one dollar and a half a day while the Hotels charge three or four dollars and we are just as comfortable as I want to be. I drew 2 months pay to day and bought a new suit of clothes and now I feel something like a white man.

I made an application this morning for a leave of absence for 30 days and I expect to be home in the course of 3 or 4 days.

We left Danville on the 19th of this Month and stopped in Richmond untill the morning of the 22d. On our arrival at Richmond I found 2 boxes filled with Clothing and grub for me and the way we went into the eatables while we were in Libby was a caution.[1]

Mother I am very anxious indeed to hear from you all and wish you to write or Telagraph to me (as soon (as you get this) as possibly I may get it if you write before I leave here.

I have lots of yarns to tell you Mother but will wait untill I get home as I cant do justice to the darn Rebs, in a letter.

You cant imagine how I want to see you and Mattie and the children and all the rest.

Good Night Mother give my love to all

G. W. Whitman

Direct Officers Hospital Anapolis Md

[Mrs. Whitman wrote the following note on the page before she forwarded George's letter to Walt:]
Walter i should have sent you this letter from George but

---

[1] Walt Whitman's notebook for February 13, 1865, contains the following entry: "Wrote to Capt. Mason, enclosing $28, for box of provisions he purchased & sent to George from City Point" (*Glicksberg*, p. 181).

thought of course you knew all about his arrival at Anapolis
i saw his name in the times with 5008 others arrived) my
not hearing from you we thought you had gone there to
see him the letter was missent to boston so it was some
days before i got it i expect him home every hour i am
very sorry indeed you did not know he was exchanged) Jeffy
has gone to Wheeling he was so delayed in getting there
Matty had a letter from him yesterday saying he would
not be able to come to Washington till after he come back but
will surely come you dont write Walt how you are whether
you are well or any thing about your affairs write all about
things we are all pretty well except sis she has a very bad
could and is not well

no more
L Whitman[1]

Head Quarters Prince St. Military
Prison Alexandria Va. May 8th 1865

Dear Mother

I arrived here and joined the Regiment about ten days
ago and was placed in command of this Prison.

I am very well, indeed but have plenty to do as I have
about 300 Prisoners (mostly thieves, Bounty jumpers and
Deserters) to look after. I have 100 of the men of our
Regt. and 5 Officers here with me guarding the Prisoners.

There is about 20 Rebel Officers here (Paroled Prisoners) but they are used very different from what we were,
when we were in Rebeldom.

I saw Walt when I came through Washington, and I
hear he was over to see me yesterday but did not find me.
Well Mammy the war seems to be over, and I think the

[1] Several other letters from George were used by Mrs. Whitman to send
a note on to Walt. The present is a sample.

most of us will soon be sent home. It is now getting late (after Eleven O clock at night) and as I feel rather tired I will go through the Prison and see that all is right and then turn in. I sleep here in the building (I have a very good room) and take my meals at a Boarding house I pay 6 dollars per week for grub but dont live any of the best.

Good night to all.

Direct Capt G. W. Whitman

Comdng Prince St Military Prison Alexandria Va

Camp of 51st Regt. N. Y. V. Vols
near Alexandria Va July 14th/65

Dear Brother.

I returned to the Regt last night (I have been away on Court Martial you know) and found your letter of July 5th and Mothers, and Hannahs, that you sent me at the same time. Poor Hann I feel quite worried about her and have just written to her saying that Mother and I will come on to see her in the cours of three or four weeks. Walt I suppose you know that we are going to be Mustered out of service, we are making out the Muster Rolls now, and we expect to be in New York in about 10 days. I have been over to Washington two or three times since I saw you, but it was always in the afternoon (after C. M. hours) so that I could not get up to your place in time to see you. Walt come over and see us, the stage leaves Willards twice every day, and brings you right to Camp, so jump in and come over. I have written to Mother to day to let her know that I am coming home, and telling her to get ready for a trip to Vermont. I am sleepy so good night Walt.

G. W. W.

The trouble about the informality of Muster is all right

Letters Written by Louisa Van Velsor Whitman

Trent Collection catalogue, page 62, number 16. From the fairly large number of letters by Whitman's mother in the Trent Collection the following have been chosen for publication with the purpose of adding to existing information on the poet's family and with the idea of illustrating the interest in politics and reading which Mrs. Whitman also shared. All are addressed to Walt. In supplying the dates we have put a question mark after the year whenever we have been unable to prove conclusively the correctness of our assignment, and to facilitate reading we have spaced Mrs. Whitman's sentences or sentence fragments.

In accounting for Walt Whitman's democratic ideas the fact has been too infrequently stressed that the poet was reared in the midst of the greatest democratic institution known to mankind—a large family. The center of it, until he himself took over, was his mother, born in 1795, married in 1816, and thirty-nine years later left a widow with eight children. One other child had died as an infant in 1825. The perfection of character which her son found in her was tested to the full by the thousand ills inherited by human flesh, especially during the period of the Civil War. Edward, her youngest son, was feeble-minded and crippled, possibly as a result of an early attack of scarlet fever. Jesse, her oldest son, had fallen from the mast of a ship and after being hospitalized for six months seemed to have recovered, but in 1860 overt signs of insanity developed, and at last his attacks became so violent that in December, 1864, he was committed to an asylum. Andrew, another son, a joiner by trade, who lived not far away with his wife Nancy and two little boys, was taken into the army but was soon discharged, to die in 1863 of a throat ailment, leaving his wife pregnant. As is evident in some of the following letters, Nancy was incapable of caring for her children properly and soon embarked upon a career which elicited strong words from Mother Whitman.

Jeff, with whose family Mrs. Whitman shared a house during the war years, had his salary from the Brooklyn Water Works reduced from ninety to fifty dollars a month in October, 1863, shortly after his second child was born. To cap the climax, he was soon thereafter drafted and had to provide funds for a substitute. Another son, George, as has been seen, volunteered early in the war, was wounded and captured, and almost constantly saw so much action that Walt in his letters to his mother tried to prepare her for news of his death. Mary, the elder daughter, seems to have prompted no special worries, but such was far from being the case with her younger sister Hannah, who suffered from a constant series of ailments, including nervous prostration, and lived a life of marital battling with her husband, Charles L. Heyde. And, finally, Walt himself began to exhibit alarming symptoms of "bad spells in the head," following soon after an infection had developed in a cut on the hand.

Yet, with seven of her eight children providing grounds for anxiety, Mother Whitman was able to sympathize with the countless soldiers whose tragic sufferings her son in Washington described in his wound-dresser letters, and Jeff could help raise funds for their relief. More than one member of the Whitman family had noble luster in his eyes—and the following letters, humble as they are, will perhaps demonstrate the fact.

[November, 1863?]
friday night most 10 oclock

Dear Walt   here goes another of mothers scientific letters when i get desperate i write   commit it to paper as you literary folk say   well i am rather better of my cold but my coughf still hangs on   it always does   when i get A cold

it seems as if i should never get clear of it but i am better
this has been a trying day mat has company Mr and Mrs
Ruggles and bothe the young ones has been musical i tell
you the little one we had down here till she expanded her
lungs merrily poor mat she a roasting beef for for supper
and all the fixings i have not been up stairs but assisted
what i could below i suppose i should have gone up but i
have a sore foot that i cant wear any but an old sleep shoe
i have a bunion on my foot which i thought would be very
troublesom but mrs brown[1] gave me some ointment to day
and it has eased it very much so i guess it will be well in a
day or two) well walt i will tell how my daily routine without any variations i get up in the morning and not very
early between 6 and 7 and make a fire and sweep out and
get some coffee and bread and butter butter is 36 cents per
lb dear eating aint it wel by this time Andrew comes lays
down part of the time but stays all day untill dark eats his
dinner here and then edd goes round for his medicine and
when he goes home at night Jess or edd goes with him and
takes his supper and probably all the rest and that aint
all we have Jimmy[2] here too) to night i sent half loaf fresh
bread with a lot of flour to make some more if nancy feels
disposed) and matty sent roast beef baked quinces apple
sauce and parsnips Andrew eats better than he has done he
looks very thin but he says his throat is a little better) then
add to that i have hatty of coarse and she is very obstropo-
lous and her uncle Andrew says if she was his hed break her
neck so you see walt what we go through every day sundays
and all you know Andrew always was testy and jelous i
think sometimes i wish i was a hundred miles off i asked

[1] The Browns lived in the same house with Mrs. Whitman. The Jefferson
Whitmans occupied the upper floor.
[2] Andrew Whitman and his wife Nancy had two children, "Jimmy" and
"Georgy."

him to day what nancy was dooing if she was dooing any
sewing he said georgy was so troubeso whether she was
always so or we know more about her i dont know but i
think she is about the lazeyest and dirtiest woman i ever
want to see she come round here to put a blister on andrews
neck i gave her a pair of trowsers to make jim a pair i said
will you make them for the child is not not comfortable with
those thin trowsers on i made him a pair myself of woolen
but i dont know why she dont let him wear them shes as
ugly as she is dirty i dont wonder he used to drink i cant
begin to tell you walt it frets me very much she at home all
day having a good time with the rent and all paid and mat
and me dooing every thing to make him comforta when i
gave her the trowsers i said have you any thread so i give
her thread to make them and i dont believe she has done any
thin to them he[3] is doctoring with dr Brody he has had
2 or 3 blisters on his neck and chest and been leeched i hope
he will get better he certainly can eat better matty makes
him a nice pudding or custard nearly every day i dont know
how we can get along with it all this winter every kind of
provition is so very dear i pity Andrew very much but i
think sometimes how much more those poor wounded and
sick soldiers suffer with so much patience poor souls i think
much about them and always glad to hear you speak of
them i dont think walt after you being amongst them so
long you could content yoursel from them it becomes a kind
of fasination and you get attached to so many of the poor
young men
O i am so afraid the rebels will get the better of Burny[4] i
hope he will be ready for them sometimes i think i wish
mead was removed but i know so little about it but the army

[3] Andrew.
[4] General Ambrose E. Burnside. Reference is later made to General George
G. Meade, then commanding the Army of the Potomac.

of the potomac seems to me to always be a little too late)
i doo hope George will reman where he is   will they get
paid soon doo you think walt   i hope he will send me enoughf
to not take any from the bank   i have given Andrew so
much   i gave him the 2 dollar you sent   i wish walt if you
could help them a little now and then   we have got to sup-
port them untill he gets better if he ever does   now i must
write about the babes   well the little baby is well and fat
and prettyer than hatty⁵   she grows tall and not so fat as
she was   she goes to jamaca with her father   O walt dont
you never hear from hann   it is so strange she never writes
i got your letter yesterday money and all   walt you might
almost write a book from this letter.

[December 4, 1863]
friday night

My dear Walt   i write to night some of the particulars
of Andrews death   he failed from the time on the morning
you left   had very bad turnes and would then revive and
be better   that night you left i was there and likewise
mary   he was very restless and did not want mary to leave
him   i stayed late   the 2 young men that came to watch
he told mary he was dying and he could not dye with
them there   they insisted on my coming home   i came and
mary stayed untill late and she came and left nancy and them
to take care of him   wendsday morning she went round   he
was very bad and sent the children here   i went again and
marthe went   he wanted her to come   she was there nearly
all day   only came home to nurse the baby   when she or
mary went to come away he would becon for them too him
that they would come back   he wanted to be mooved from

---

⁵ Jessie and Mannahatta were the daughters of Thomas Jefferson and
Martha Whitman.

the lounge to the chair he wanted mothers rocking chair
poor soul he died in it wendsday night martha was there
till late then she came home and mary and Jeffy staid all
night wensday he wanted to see Jeffy marthe went to the
office for him he came and stayed till toward night and came
home and had som tea i went again in the evening and came
back for to see to the childre as i said before and martha and
Jeffy went this was wendsday night they had to fan him
all night and bathe him in brandy nance went to bed when
she came out in the morning she brought such a smell that
Jeffy got sick and had to come home being up all night and
shortly after mary came bringing georgy besmeard from
head to foot mary said she could not go again the smell
and her throat being so bad so i sent Jess around till they
had their breakfast Jeffy and mary thought he could be
moved round here we sent for the doctor he went round
to see and came back and said he thought we might but we
must doo it very soon mat went round behind the doctor
and staid till he came and told us we could he said he
would probably live untill 10 oclock that night this was
thursday morning mary went back and Jeff and mrs brown
when the doctor spoke of it nancy made a great adue said
you shant have him he belongs to me he said he wished
he could dye now i suppose it hurt him mrs brown came
for me i went before i got there mary said he would look
around she asked him if it was mother he wanted he
mooved his head i am very glad we dident doo any thing
about mooving him i am thankfu we was all there he died
like any one going to sleep without a struggle sensible to
the last just before he died he turned his head and looked
at your and georges pictures for some time and then shut his
eyes god grant i may never witness another) he seemed
as if he was satisfied that we were all around him he drank

without choaking before he died   he was laid out there and
brought here last night and lays in mrs browns room without
waches   is to be buried to morro at 2 oclock   mary has gone
away this afternoon   he looks very natural   his friends is
all dooing very good Cornell[1] in particular   i order three
carriages and cornell will send one for her and the childr   he
is laid in a frock coat of Georges and vest and every thing
very respetcful   plate on his coffin with his age and name
Jeffy will write the rest   i am composed and calm   would
not wish him back to suffer   poor soul i hope he is at rest
i have not heard from George since you left   i wish i could
write to hannah   walter tell her if she could have seen the
sufferings of her poor brother she would be thankfull he was
out of his agony)   write to me walter as soon as you can
if i best take money from the bank to pay the expences   i told
the undertaker i would settle it in the course of 2 weeks)
one thing more i must say mrs brown could not be kinder
than she is   i shall always respect her for her great kindness
in our affliction   what i am going to write h[?]   i would say
nothing only i thin Jeffy will   last night marthe sent Jess
around with nancy tea and seeing his brothers corps seemed
to effect him very much   he had not ought to been sent   he
took on very much and looked a little strange when he came
back but nothin more[2]   seemed to be very sad but this afternoon martha and hattie and sis were down here hattie done
something he dident like   he got up and with a vengeanc to
whip her and marthe forbad him to touch her child   there
was a scene   he called her very bad names and looked very
wild for a while   i told marthe to go up stairs or not say any
thing but she would   she began to cry and her back pained

---

[1] Possibly James Cornell, mentioned also on p. 196. In the Brooklyn
Daily Times for Sept. 9, 1857, Whitman published a sketch which mentions
a Justice Cornwell of the Police Court (*Uncollected*, II, 10-12).

[2] Jesse Whitman was insane.

her [w]hen she went up stairs of course Jeff had to hear it all in the strongest light i should said nothing about it but Jeff said he should write to you to morrow i said Jesse your brothe lies up stairs dead he calmd down immediately and is very good natured i think it was going there last night that affected him)   write how you are walt and all good night there was a very good little peice in the eagle last night about you[3] Jeffy will i think send it to you   this is a pachd letter   good bye again

your mother   L W

[March 5, 1865]
Sunday night

dear Walt   George has come home came this morning he looks quite thin and shows his prison life[1] but feels pretty well considering what he suffered he was very sick at one time i think it was in january with the lung fever he was six weeks in the hospital so bad that the doctor thought he would die this doctor i think he calls his name wilson seems to have taken A liking to him and did what he could for him he had no medicine blistered him and gave him mercury he was dilirious and lay in A stupor till the night the fever turned he says he felt A thrill run through him and thought he was dying he was in the dark he cald to one of the nurses to bring A light and to raise him up and give him a piece of paper and pencil and he wrote to me that was his last night and what was due him from the goverment and told the man to blow out the light and go to bed and he said he shut his eyes and never expected to open them

[3] The article dealt with Whitman as a well-known citizen of Brooklyn who was acting as a nurse in Washington.

[1] For George's attempts to disguise the hardships of his imprisonment, see his letter on p. 179. Much of the substance of the present letter has been published in *Glicksberg*, p. 181 n.

again and went to sleep and when he awoke he was all in a
sweat and just at daylight one of the officials of the place
came very softly to take all he had in his pockets they
thought he would be dead he says he has seen them before
the poor fellows is dead turn their pockets inside out and
take all when the doctor came in the morng he says you
are better he said it was his constitution that saved him he
lay on the flour two or three days before he went to the
hospital he had no drawers and only A thin pair of flanne
trowsers and no shirt part of the time they stole his things
it seems awful to think of but he is got home when they
were captured they dident give them any thing to eat from
friday morng till sunday when he was captured he had 100
dl they searched him 3 times and he saved his money he
cut A place in his neck tie and put 50 d bill in and put some
in his tobacco and some silver in his mouth one next to
him they took 600 dl from they took all sam pooleys[2]
George says sam would fared poorley if it hadent been for
him he cooked what they could get and george provided
he says that beans kept them alive they would get A quart
and cook them without any thing he brought home a piece
of the corn bread how they lived on it i cant see they
would have nothing else for six weeks at A time i sent
Georges letter yesterday as soon as i got yours i had no
idea but what you see Georges name amongst the arrived
Georg says there was 20 yesterday died at anapolus some
died eating they were he says like hungry woolvs had got
so famished i told him to day to not think any more about
it he has pains in his legs effects of the fever Jeffy is not
home yet and sis is not well yet she seems to have A kind
of fever write walt when you get this i feel better than i

---

[2] Sam Pooley was a fellow-officer with George in the Fifty-first New York
Volunteers. Walt had used his influence to arrange for a special exchange of
George and Pooley (*ibid.*, p. 180).

have felt   the rest is all well   i thought you would like to hear something about his prison life   L W

tuesday noon Nov 14 [1865]

My dear Walt
    i have waited and waited to hear from you and have got no word from you since you left which seems so strange that i feel quite uneasy for fear something is the matter   i may get a letter this afternoon but i cant conceeve why i have not heard from you   you are so prompt to write and i wanted so to hear of your safe arrival   it is very warm here to day uncomfortably so   Edd has been quite sick with his eye and face all swoln up so he could not see   he has taken some medicine and is some better to day   Walt where is all the Drum taps   we have looked all over for one or two   i thought you left some up stairs but cant find one   i had one of the first ones on the table here and i cant find it   i used to read some in it almost every night before i went to Bed   you must write just as quick as you get this no more but see [?]   your mothe
                                                        L W
did you get the paper the new yorker

[February 25, 1868]
tuesday

well Walt we have lived to see something that never was i suppose known before in america the impeachment![1]   i think it rather sad but notwithstanding exactly as it should be   i suppose the excitement at washington is far greater than here   the copperheads here is all for fight that a war will be the result   some great politician down town wanted to bet yesterday that the impeachment would not take place

[1] The formal impeachment of Andrew Johnson began on Feb. 25, 1868.

so our georgey took him up told him he would bet him that
andew Johnso would be impeaed in ten hours from that
time   the gentleman backed down after putting his hand in
his pocket to take out his money   george came home on
sunday morning very unexpected as i dident look for him
till next saturday   he came something about the iron of the
pipes he rejected as unfit)   i got your letter walter yesterday monday with 5 dollars   i was glad to have it walt but
i doo think sometimes you send me more than you can afford
and more than i ought to expect   but mamma appreciates it
if she dont make many [illegible]   walt you wrote about
your peice in an english magazine that you got 50 d in gold[2]
its first rate to handle gold in these days but i want to know
what peice it was   i thought of every one and could not make
out what peice it was   when you write again i wish you would
tell me all about it but the gold is quite a new thing to be
paid in these days)   i think we will get the galaxy and see
Oconor peice[3]   if its as stupid as his others i dont think it will
be worth 25 cts   i dont see into his writing such peices as he
writes   i should think him capable of writing something more
substancial a man that can converse as he can   well davis
was here last sunday   he gave a good account of the St louis
folks   he says Jeff is much better there than here   it agrees
with him better and he thinks matty will be all right when
they get settled   he says they all felt the effects of the change
of climate   its affect is a kind of diarea   he says he thinks
matty will like it better there than here when they get to
housekeeping   it is in the neighborhood of general Shermans
house that was presented to him) and a nice school near   he
davis looks very well indeed   says he is very glad he went

[2] Probably "Whispers of Heavenly Death," published in the *Broadway*,
N.S., I, 21-22 (Sept., 1868).
[3] W. D. O'Connor's satirical poem, "The Ballad of Sir Ball," appeared
in the *Galaxy*, V, 328-333 (March, 1868).

out there that he and Jeff has worked very hard but have got through the worst of it   aint it been cold Walt   i gess it has been stinging here but its quite moderate to day)   i have heard nothing from aunt fanny   i suppos she is living yet) the last speech of Stephens[4] that was read before the impeamen was good very indeed)   i am pretty well   good bye walt dear

[March 13, 1868]
friday afternoon
Dear Walt   i have just got your letter with 2 dol and the paper   i have not read it yet but shall this afternoon   i had to write to tell you what i had done   i couldent feel contented till i did   well i havent committed any crime but i have spent the money order you sent me for something i have always wanted but never was able to get   well i have got a lounge   it was quite cheap and good hair cloth but after i got it i thought i hadent ought to spent the money but now i have told you i shall feel better but i have got a little money left besides the 2 dolls you sent me to day   i thought i would be saving and george was gone so i would get it so walt i can get along if you send me about 2 dollars next week   i am glad you are going to have new cloths   i dont see how you doo to make your cloths last so long   george is getting something every month)   i gess this is the last peice of furniture i shall get   i always wanted a lounge   now i have got one   i had a letter from Jeff   i beleeve i told you Davis was here tuesday evening and he and Baynton his partner in jersey is to come here this afternoon   that is the cause of my not reading the paper   i have been baking some bread and cake as davis goes away to night so i thought he would probably stay to tea   i seem to have quite a number call to see me   among the number was Ellen vanwyck   she

[4] Thaddeus Stevens.

says she liked you and would like to see you   she is quite out of health   she stayed and had a cup of tea)   ann van-wyk sister Ester i dont think you ever saw her she married a man by the name of J baylis   he had a farm when they were married but drinked and sported it all away and they now live here in great poverty   he has been in the hospitall he got drunk and was took to the station house and he tryed to cut his throat but dident succeed

John varny helps her i beleeve   but so it is every one has their troubles)   you go i see walt to mrs Borroughs yet how does mrs Oconor and she get along   mrs Oconor thought they would not perhaps   i told her she must doo like mrs black   when the woman up stairs said she woulden live with children mrs black told her they would get along nicely)

George and i was talking about if the impeachment was carried if it would make any change with you   we thought speed would be the one that would take the place of stans-bury)[1]   doo you know walt i have always felt a kind of sadness when i read the articles of impeac   not but what i always thought he was bad but there is so many things to be considered)   i sent and got the sun to see how the election went friday afternoon   my love to mrs and mr Oconor and mrs and mr Borroughs

[May 14, 1868?]
thursday

My dear Walt   i write to tell you that janey maquire that is nanc brothers wife has been here and tells me awfull things of the wreched creature   she[1] has had twins   one is

---

[1] Henry Stanbery, Attorney-General in Johnson's cabinet, resigned on March 12, 1868, to act as chief counsel for Johnson. James Speed had already served as Attorney-General under Lincoln. Walt, it should be remembered, was working as a clerk in the office of the Attorney-General.

[2] Andrew Whitman's widow, Nancy.

dead the other is living and the children is sent out to beg
by the day and her brother—the one to the court house wants
to get the 3 children away from her and have them put in
some institution) what i want you to doo Walter dear
is this to write a letter to James cornell for him to intercede
in getting them from her she drinks and every thing else
thats bad) tell Justice cornell for (Andrew's sake for
heavens sake to doo what he can) i wish you would say
to him that the home of the friendless in new york is a good
institution half orphan children can be got in there without
pay) Janey says if they are put in the brooklyn institution
they have to pay something that eddward maquire that is
the wretches brother will pay for two if we will pay for
one but they i think if the proper way is taken can be got
in new york she said she couldent tell me how bad things
were that if the children can be got away from her they
never will countenance her she said her brother Jim that
is another brothe of nancee would have shot her he was so
enbitter Eddwar is the one with one arm keeps the new
court house and his wife Janey said to day it affected him
so that it made him sick the money you left for the children
and her we could never find her Edd went to look for
her and she had mooved) i told Janey to day about the
money and for her to take it and get something for them
she said she would come here again soon that it was no use
to get any thing now nance pawn every thing i hope you
will write to cornell walter
i am midling well only lame
the maquires is very respectable men

June 25 [1868?]
Dear Walt i received your letter to day thursday with
the money all right i thought it was a goner as i dident

get it yesterday i couldent hardly give it up yesterday
as you wrote in your fridays letter i would get your letter
on wensday but it come to day very welcom Mr Burrows
has not been to see me i was exspecting him every day
after you wrote but he dident come) i have not heard
from Jeff nor matty since i wrote last to you) edd said
the letter man asked him to day why his mother dident get
any more letters i used to get so many matty used to write
quite often and Jeffy once in a while but they have all
seemed to fall off.) but the good old standby if he should
fail me i should have nothing to look for but i gess there is
no danger is there walter dear as long as you have your old
mamma i often think how loth many is to have children
and what would become of me if i had none Janey Mcclure[1]
that is nancs brothers wife was here the other day she came to
see if cornell had been to see me about the children she
sends them the most saucy letters they think if they should
doo any think she would not be any too good to kill her
brother Edd Thats the one in the new court house) i have
come to the conclusion there is but one way to doo and that
is to send them to the nursery to flatbush there is no insti-
tutio in the city that they would be taken as they are Janey
thinks that is the only place that she couldent get them out
i cant begin to tell and i dont want too half the worse that
wreched woman does i dont know walter how you feel
about their being taken there but i know that i should feel
much better than to have them sent out begging it would
be no disgrace as there is many there that is of good parent-
age there they would be clothed and fed if they ever can
be cleaned Janey says the are so dirty that you would not
know they were ever cleand good by walter dear

your mother

[1] In the preceding letter Mrs. Whitman gave the name as "Maquire."

i am about the same as usual   feel quite smart at time   they
are digging the cellar at georges lot   he had it survayed
yesterday

[August 19, 1868?]
wensday evening

My dear Walt   i received your letter yesterday as usual
it was all right and am glad to hear you are feeling pretty
well and every thing goes on pretty well with you   you
are so attached to washington i dont beleive you ever would
be contented any where else   i dont wonder at it for
i think you have more true friends there than any other
place)   i mean those not related to you of course)   i suppose
it makes you feel awkard to go to mr Oconors their not
being friendly and you being friendly to both but when
they move it will be different   its very disagreable to
live in one house and not be on speaking terms   i should
think the oconors was the last people to fall out with)   well
Walt here we are yet in the same old place but i doo want
to get out of it very much indeed there is so many children
and not the best i ever see but a continual traveling up and
down from morning till night   one good thing their dog is
dead   he filled the house with fleas   so maybe well get
clear of them now)   george says we must stay here till the
1 of october and then he see what arrangements he can
make with smith to take the house all himself and then we
shall move there this winter   i shall be glad enoughf   maybee they will settle it up before   i told george i wanted to
move before you came home but walter dear if it suits you
better to come before that time you must come but i thought
i should be so lonesome when i got away from this rabble
that i should want you to come then and stay your full
month)   george has been to florence to the foundry to get

some big pipe they fell short and he dont have much to
doo now he talks of going up on the island for a day or
two) florence is the foundry where Jeff has his pipe made
when george got there Jeffs inspector was out gunning
george left word for him to come to the hotel it was some
pipe that Jeff had they wanted for this main so when the
young man came they told him mr whitman wanted to see
he was quite alarmed he thought of course it was Jeff
george thought he was very glad as he dident care for Jeff
to find him out gunning) george has got a draft from Jeff
for 510 dols and got the money without any trouble) now
walter dear dont wait till we move if it suits you i make a
good deal of rectoning of your coming i feel pretty well at
present

[February, 1869?]

My dear Walter   i got your letter all safe to day wensday
it was rather late but it come yesterday was a tremendous
rain the water has been a foot deep in the cellar they say
the rats has undermined it but it has dried away some its a
low place the water settles in the yard it is better georg
sold it they are much pleased with it say they wouldent
take 1000 dols for their bargain mrs steers gets along very
well with her bakery) we have had mrs Black here she
has just gone and quite a releef it is too she come she said
to tell me of a sure cure for the rheumatis i asked her what
it was she said put a potato in each pocket and wear them
in your pocket till they are hard and the rheumatis will
i supos go in the potato she asked me when she went away
if i would doo it i told her i would carry half a dozen
if they would do me any good
well walt i am glad you are bettr of your distress in your
head very many people is complaining of colds well the

president cant pardon very many more roages you know i
suppose Devlin is pardoned[1] the papers say peirpont[2] is to
be the attorney genrall but i suppos you will know soon
i hear from Jeff and mat once in a while Jeff has or has
had great anxiety about the works the river rises so much
higher that usual that there is fear of the overflowing of
the works poo Jeff i expect he is in lots of trouble but as
we understood Davis it wouldent doo such an amount of
damage if it did overflow but Jeff is so nervous)
walter dear if you can as well as not i wish you would send
me the draft next week) George had to make a payme
the other day and had to take all he had to make it out)
give my love to the oconors and love to yourself)

Louisa Whitm

31 march [1869?]

Well Walt here comes another letter Edd says hes tired
carrying letters yesterday i wrote one to mary and one to
hanna i promised mary if i heard any thing from hanna i
would write to her she wanted very much to see Heydes
letters but i told her they would only excite her and make her
feel bad that i dident put any faith in what he wrote they
are very insulting but i take them from whence they came i
wish han was something like young chappells wife up stairs
here he is awfull at times wishes to god he could find
her dead when he come home she dont know i suppose i
hear him swear at her the other night he made a great
noise i thought he had knocked her down but i gess he
dident the next day she was singing and lively as usual she

---

[1] John Devlin, a Brooklyn merchant convicted on Feb. 3, 1868, in a
Federal court in New York for the illegal sale of liquor, was pardoned early
in 1869 by President Johnson.

[2] Edwards Pierrepont, to whom Mrs. Whitman probably refers, was in
1868 appointed U. S. attorney for the New York district, but later became a
U. S. Attorney-General.

says he has an awful temper but it goes in one ear and out the other   her mother lives in brooklyn   has her second husband   she was in my room the other day   she said Janey deserved a better lot that her father was a minester   i think they are from the south but Janey gives as much back as she gets   she goes to her mother and stays a week or two edd says he told him he liked to be alone)   well walter i have the whisper of heavenly death   it lays here on the table by my side   i have read it over many times and have had one person ask me to let her take it hom   i said no i would rather not let it go out of my hands and am very glad i did so as you wish me to reserve it   i felt as if i should preserve it for i liked it   it was so solemn)   i got your letter walter this day with 2 dols   i am feeling better to day my head dont pain me and have got rid of the dissiness   i am glad to have george home on some accounts   i have more work to doo but probably its best)   i asked him about the lot in putman & he said his price was 1000 dols but if you would like to buy it you could have it for 700[1]   that is what it cost him   he was up there last sunday   he said there was three houses on that side about 15 feet from the old shop three story frame houses very good all different as if they were built by the ones that would ocupy them and 6 acrost the street)   george says with a high fence the side of the shop he dont think it would be so very bad   i only wish we had a house on it   it would be a home any how   its astonishing how houses rents   there was a place in clermont george went to see about but it was taken   the uper part 30 dol per month

24 [March 1870]

O walt aint it sad to think the poor soul hadent a friend

---

[1] Walt planned to build a house for his mother and himself, but the plan never came to fruition.

near him in his last moments and to think he had a paupers grave[1] i know it makes no difference but if he could have been buried decently but hes done poor fellow i was thinking of him more lately than common i wish walter you would write to Jeff and hanna that he is dead i will write to george i feel very sad of course walt if he has done ever so wrong he was my first born but gods will be done good bie walter dear walter send me one envelope next time you write

[March 28, 1870]
monday

My dear walt i received your letter and paper with jesse death in it poor soul i hope hes better off but it makes me feel very sad dident the doctor say any thing about how long he was sick before he died walter has doctor chappin left the institution i see it wasent his name that sent you the letter i dident write to George as he will be home friday or saturday he aint very busy now i am sorry walt you have a cold doo you have them dissy spells you had home i shall be glad when it comes time for you to come home i have had a letter from matty she is quit smart says the children is making reckoning of your coming out there[1] walter i did want the envelopes with your name on i havent one martha used them to write to you when she was here or i shouldent be out) walter dear you needent send the order this week next week will doo) you may send the papers this week if conveinent
we have had great havoc here in brooklyn with the storm

---

[1] Jesse Whitman, "a seafaring man," died in Kings County Lunatic Asylum on March 21, 1870. Apparently because of a delay in communicating with the family representative, Walt, he was buried in the potter's field. For further information on Jesse Whitman, see Molinoff, *Some Notes on Whitman's Family*, pp. 19-23.

[1] St. Louis, Missouri.

we diden feel much the effects only the smoke came down
the chimney bad by spells   it was a dreary day

your Mother

[July 12, 1870?]
tuesday

My dear Walt   i received your letter on monday   glad
to hear you get along so well   every one seems to complain so much of the weather   its hot to be shure but its no
use fretting about it   well Walt i have been to day and had
my picture taken   i have been saving money for it for this
2 months and to day i have been to pendletons on the corner
of fulton and Johnson st and had six larges ones taken   i
went alone   i told the man i wanted very extraordinary ones
for the were to go to a distance and he said he would take
the best that could be taken   i set three times   the last one
did look very good   the others was good only the eyes
wasent so good   they will cost nearly 20 dollar   yours and
georges i will have framed and one for myself   i shall send
han one in the package   so you see walt i bequeath something
to my children so they will not forget me)   i hear nothin
from Jeff and matt   maybee they are away)   good bie
walter dear   i will give the book to helen[1]

tuesday morning Oc 10   [1871?]
My dear walt   i had company yesterday so i dident write
to you   we had aunt freeloves daughter elizabeth with an
other lady here yesterday   i got your letter this morning and
i got three last week   i dont know what i would doo walt if
it wasent for you to think of me   it seems as if all the other
sons and daughters has their own to attend to which is perfectly natural)   george and loo[1] and Jeff insists on my

[1] Probably Helen Price, who from time to time visited Mrs. Whitman.
For Walt's friendship with the Price family, see *Glicksberg*, pp. 106 ff.
[1] George Whitman married Louisa Orr Haslorn on April 14, 1871.

breaking up houskeeping   they dident only insist but almost commanded me   i told them i should remain here this winter if i lived)   they none of them want edd walter and they would soon get tired of paying his board and we aint much expence to any but you walter dear for any thing but houseroo   at any rate i shant break up as long as i can get around   if i lose the use of my limbs altogether then i wont object   i suppose they do it for the best   they think i live so lonesome)   but walt dont worry about me breaking up   i have had my way as edd says to long)

i had a letter from loo since they went home   Jimmy² behaved very well while they was away but after they got home he stayed out late and on wensday night he was out all night   he went to a political meeting and the band of music atracted him   he said he slept in the alley but loo seems to have great patience with him   she said he took on and cried and promis to not do so any more   he would only be a good boy)

walt i have a poem by Jean Bruce Washburn³ of the yo semite valley california mrs stantons aunt   i think its beautiful   its a small pamphlet   i will send it to you if you wish walter   write walter if you would like it   the old indian tradition i think is so beautifu   the fire in the woods on the praires is awful to read

[1873]¹

my dearly beloved walter   thank god i feel better this morning   i hope i shall be better now   my rheumatism is better in my limbs   whether its that or what has affected

---

² Apparently George and Louisa had taken Nancy's son "Jimmy" in charge.
³ *Yo Semite. A Poem*, San Francisco, 1871.

---

¹ This letter was written at the home of the George Whitmans in Camden, N. J. All of the preceding letters by Louisa Whitman were written from Brooklyn. Mrs. Whitman died on May 23, 1873.

my head i cannot tell but my head and my very brain has seemed to be affected   but i feel better this morning and hope i shall be better still   when i feel so bad i want so much to be with you walter dear   george and Lou has been kind to me   good bie   i think we would be happier if we was together walter dear   we will live saving and i hope i shall be well enoughf to see to things   eddy is very good boy lately   he says he hopes i wont die   good bie my dear walt   i have got your good letter dear walt

Letters Written by
Mary Elizabeth Van Nostrand

*Trent Collection catalogue, pages 61-62, numbers 13 and 14.
Walt's older sister, Mary Elizabeth (1821-1899), was married
at the age of nineteen to a shipwright, Ansel Van Nostrand,
and lived in the whaling village of Greenport, Long Island,
where she reared five children: George, Fanny, Louisa, Ansel,
and Minnie. The two following letters are filled with gossip
about her own brood or about her husband's relatives and show
once again how much the Whitmans owed for family information to the sustaining interest of the invalid poet.*[1]

Dear Mother   Greenport Feb 16 [1867?]
    I suppose you think strange that I have not come but
I will tell you how it is   I expected to come last monday but
we got a dispatch monday to come immediately to farming-
dale as they did not think Grandmother would be alive when
we got there   so Ansel went and I thought I should go
next day but when he got there I she had revived up so I
did not go   Ansel came back yesterday   he says she cannot
live so I think I will wait and see before I come as Ansel
wants I should   but dont fret I shall come soon.   We are
all well but we have had a very severe winter in G Port and
I think it will snow again before night but I hope not   We
all went sleighriding last saturd to riverhead 22 miles and
had a good time.   I had a letter from George yesterday   he
is not in any business yet but his wife is so he is all right
Louisa and John are well and getting along nicely. but I
will tell you all the news when I come   I hope dear mother

[1] The little that is known about Mary appears in Molinoff, *Some Notes
on Whitman's Family*, pp. 3-9.

you are well this winter and if you should want me before
I come why write and you will see molly quick   I dont
hardly know what is the matter with grandmother   she has
had the rheumatism very bad this winter and I guess she is
all run down and Ansel says grandfather is miserable too   he
dont think he will stay long in this country either   Pheby
has got almost 5 young ones and it is a perfect bedlam there
it is a bad place to be sick.   Ansel expects to go fishing east
again and I suppose we shall be alone and I want you to
come and make us a good long visit.   I suppose you hear
from Mat how is she getting along.   I dont believe she
will be as much pleased as she anticipated

I think I have written you quite a letter so I will close

Your affectionate daughter
Mary

Greenport Mar 16 [1878?]

Dear dear brother

Again I am ashamed of myself for not writing to you
before as I have received so many letters from you and
always think I will answer but one thing and another keeps
me from it so now I will try to tell you about myself   well
we jog along in about the old way   sometimes it is nip and
tuck with us   sometimes nips ahead and sometimees tuck but
in the main we are all right as long as I only have my health
Ansel has been out of work for a year but has work now so
we are all right   I often hear from you through the papers
and am glad enough to think you are better this winter and
hope and pray you will entirely recover and believe you
will and would like very much to see you whenever you feel
as if you could come or any of the rest of my folks and will do
all I can to make it pleasant for them   Our family of children
live here around us   Minnie has three children and Fanny

one the rest have none Greenport is about the same as it was when you was here only improved very much and now dear brother I want to thank you for the many letters cards and papers you have sent me and likewise for the christmas present you sent in the letter and want you to write when ever you can for you are the only one now since dear Mother left us that ever writes a word to me Please when you write again mention how Eddy and hannah Jeff George and all get along as I should like to hear from them and I do think I will not be so long in answering again. I suppose you have almost forgotten how it looks here Louisa and John have built a new house opposite here and are living in it Minnie's husband has bought one a little further off and they are living in that. I dont know as this will interest you but I thought I would just write it. I feel myself growing old and failing every day but my health has been better this winter than usual

Dear Brother one more favor I would like to ask of you that is when you have time to please copy our family record[1] and send to me as I really have forgotten how old we all are

From your affectionate sister

Mary Van Nostrand

[1] Whitman inscribed the record of the family, "Births," "Marriages," and "Deaths," in a Bible which he sent to Mary as a Christmas present, 1878 (*ibid.*, pp. 6-8).

Letters Written by
Hannah Louisa Heyde

*Trent Collection catalogue, pages 60-61, numbers 6 and 9.
Hannah Louisa Heyde, four and a half years younger than
Walt, was undoubtedly the favorite sister of the Whitman boys.
In spite of "hell's own life" of domestic feud and an almost
constant succession of ailments culminating in a stroke of paralysis, she survived her husband by sixteen years and died on July
18, 1908.*

*Apparently more of a reader than most of the Whitmans,
Hannah was constantly receiving books as well as money from
her poet-brother. Nothing cheered her in her periods of illness
more than news from him, and the physician who attended her
in her last days has borne testimony to the ardent enthusiasm
with which she pronounced his name.[1]*

*The following three letters, the third addressed to Walt,
show full well the deep affection which existed between Whitman and his younger sister.*

March 20 [1867]

Dear Mother

I have just got Walts letters telling me about your arm
being lame. I feel quite uneasy, be careful as you can   you
must not get sick. Mother I always think about you like
you was when you was here   I think about you all more than
ever.   it has worried me lately at night so I could not get
asleep because I have not written.   I mean now to write every
week or two.

I never in my life see anybody so good & have so much

---

[1] Mrs. Katherine Molinoff has given a very interesting sketch of Hannah
in *Some Notes on Whitman's Family*, pp. 24 ff.

patience with me as Walt does. I cant tell you Mother how I feel about it, so I wont try. I dont know what makes him so good. I have got something that I can keep & see with the money he sent me but its the kindness I care for, and I would like him to look out for & take *good* care of himself first. What good letters you write Mother, to Walt, they tell so much about home I should miss them if Walt didint send them some times to me, its just as good as if you wrote

If you are well dear Mother cant you come here[2] this summer I should be perfectly happy. I will do anything & everything I can for you so you will have a better & pleasanter time than before, only I want you to come in May or first of June, stay till fall, now Mother dont say or think *no* till you consider & talk it over then write, do come Mother. it may do you good, I want you with all my might, it *will do me good.* I dont keep any girl but my house is neater than when you was here, I cant work hard or hurry. I am not near as strong as I used to be, Dr Thayer has advised me for a year to go home   he says I need a change, he sends his respects, he always speaks of you, he dont come in as often as he used, but is very kind, this neighborhood has changed, much you will like it better, all new people and very social, they run in often.—very clever people have bought the Barnes house, opposite, Mrs Molt, or Dolan, never comes here, I dont see Mrs Miller often.   I go out very seldom & she has a young child born a few weeks after Mr Millers death.   Mrs Miller & her mother are spiritualists, they did not allow him Mr Miller to take the Dr remedies, thought he could be cured by spiritualists, it made some talk at the time, — I want to see you all as much as ever, Maty has never sent me her's & the childrens pictures.   Will

[2] Burlington, Vermont.

George ever come to see me, he knows I want him to, I often see persons that I think looks like him. When Walt has his [vac]ation this sumer perhaps he will come [Ther]e is a little notice about Walt in the New York times, March 18 — in the European news.[3] Mother will you ask Walt to be sure continue to send me all that is published about him, I was glad to get, & much pleased with last Leaves of Grass/ Walt is spoken of pretty often here in the Burlington times,—also tell Walt I was much pleased & oblidged for the gloves & book of poetry, & other novel I have worn the gloves all winter, I dont know Mother why I dont write home & to Walt. I always mean to, dear Mother I *will write* very soon & tell you every thing. this is only a line, you cant immagine how much I do want to see you all, if I live I mean to come home, & I do want to live long enough to see you all once more. tell Walt I was glad to hear he was back in his old home. if they are new people, I was [s]orry to hear he had the neuralgie, but he is well now he says. I have been all winter trying to crochet him a scarf but did not as usual do as I mean to. I hope you are well now dear Mother. Give my love to Jeff & all I want to hear more about how Nancey[4] gets along do take good care of yourself dear Mother

Good bye   Han

I will write *soon* again, tell Walt I will use all the paper. I feel sorry & ashamed that I have been neglectful apparently, Give my love to Mary[5] I liked Walts picture that he sent

[3] A paragraph, headed "Walt Whitman," in which the correspondent calls attention to a "column of genial and appreciative criticism" of the poet in a late issue of the London *Sunday Times*. *Leaves of Grass*, the British critic observed, will hold a "prominent position in American literature," but "cannot possibly be admitted into family reading." "Whitman combines the freedom and coarseness of Rabelais, the poetry of Ossian, and the philosophic flavor of Emerson."

[4] The widow of her brother Andrew.

[5] Her older sister, Mary Van Nostrand.

[February?] 5, 1873

My dear darling Mother

We were glad to get your letter.

I was very anxious about Walt.[1]— I wanted to come where you was.

It was all I could do to stay quiet.

I think Walt will get entirely well again, for others do, I know of two persons here, that have had simular attack's, that are perfectly well

There are very few persons on earth that are loved as much as Walt so I know dear Mother he will get well,

Write as often as you can, and you must try to keep well Mother, so that Walt will not feel a bit anxious,—Give him a great deal of love, and say that I do not forget him for a instant, and that he must take great care, (more for himself) and a little on his friends acount.

You or Louisa[2] must tell us in a few days how he is.

I wish we could do something for him, that seems hard to me that we cannot.　Good bye dearest Mother

Han

Love to Lou & George) (Thanks for that gift in your letter)

Burlington Vt　Jan 24　[1892]

Only a word my darling to say how *precious precious* your *letter* is & how much I feel your thinking of me now. but my dearest you will be better & then I may write to you　you have my constant prayers & thoughts always. but my dear dear brother only get better.　there is no words to say what I feel for you　Want to send you so much love, and do feel so thankful that you are better

The $5 came safe my dear kind brother

Dear dear brother only get better again

Han

---

[1] Whitman had suffered a stroke of paralysis.
[2] Louisa ("Lou") was the wife of George Whitman.

Letters Written by
Charles L. Heyde

Trent Collection catalogue, pages 60-61, numbers 6 and 8. The most eloquent critic of Leaves of Grass among Whitman's relatives was his brother-in-law Charles L. Heyde, a painter who specialized in Vermont scenery. Walt spoke of him as "a leech"—"the bed-buggiest man on the earth"—"almost the only man alive who can make me mad."[1] The reason for the violent reaction was not Heyde's activities as a literary critic but his treatment of his wife Hannah, whom he married in 1852. The earliest letters of Heyde's in the Trent Collection show no signs of a family quarrel, for they were written during a honeymoon period in which the artist found his soul stirred by the beauties of the Vermont landscape, but as the years rolled on he found no better subject for his epistles to Mother Whitman or to Walt than the wretched health or the perverse disposition of his wife. It is clear that Hannah was not a good housekeeper and that her illnesses were a trial, but Heyde's agitation was caused also by increasing poverty and by a mental disorder, possibly aggravated by the use of alcohol, which led to his confinement in an insane asylum on October 29, 1892. There he died a few days later, aged seventy years.[2]

Most of his letters that survive are attempts to keep Walt informed about the state of Hannah's health and to acknowledge the receipt of sums of money sent from time to time by the poet. The few selected for publication here illustrate the nature of the correspondence and present the chief surviving remarks on Walt or his poems made by his artist brother-in-law.

[1] *Traubel*, III, 498-500.
[2] Molinoff, *Some Notes on Whitman's Family*, pp. 32 ff.

North Dorset [Vermont] Sept. 22, 1852

Dear Mother.

Your letter was recieved.   I have nothing new to communicate respecting this region, excepting that I made a journey to the top of the mountain, to view a famed trout pond, and a beautifull sight it was to behold so large a body of pure, transparent water at so great a height.   In the very heart of the wilderness, surrounded by fir and spruce trees, and wild shrubbery.   It contains very fine trout, which, when they are in a biting humor are taken from it in great abundance.   I caught a few and saw some very large ones. The distance up the mountain from here is about two miles, and the way is about as dark as twilight.   It is very steep of ascent, and there was no path, the way we took.   We returned safe by night and found Hannah expecting.   The weather has been very unfavourable, partly rainy and at other times windy.   I have not been able to accomplish any thing since Hannah wrote.   I must get away earlier another Season. The foliage is changing very rapidly.   I found the large canvas, I brought with me, too large and sent to New York for others; after a weeks delay, those not arriving, I sent another order, and now they have all arrived, so I have plenty of material   Hannah is well and we unite in our best wishes and regards for family and friends.

Respecting any arrangement of your house, do that allways, which is most conducive to your own advantage.

I hope Father continues well.   It will soon be time for soft shell clams.

I remain for wife and self

Affectionatey Yours

C L Heyde

Burlington May 18. 1860

Dear Walt.

Recieved your book,[1] also a letter for Han.—Feel proud myself—the copy I now have is just the thing to handle frequently—I like the poems better than those issued first. I like the portrait, it looks very much as you do at the present time. It has a little air of a foreign savan—however —but it is a good likeness.

I think that some of the poems open splendid—grandly —there is a fault or eccentricity however, in some, that is, they diverge too abruptly from a lofty theme or elevating imagery into common place—ordinary—and repulsive object, or subject matter— But they are poems of the thouroughfare of life passions and emotions of the universe and humanity—on all sides taken—as they approach and appear —without selection—symapthies utterd and communion held with all in turn and none rejected—Poems of glorious, liberal, soul filld emotion. They will be read—they must have a place—But you'l write a perfect poem one of these days, filld with nature sublimely— Your thoughts are true thoughts— Common sense is the best philosophy— Cant has too long ruled the world and judged the case of erring humanity— Your Poems are sustaining— I hope that there will be a jolly good fight over them — The public are lazy—and need some disturbance to arouse them—

Many thanks to you— We expected to have seen you here— Han is disappointed, but you have been detaind in Boston a long time— Our scenery here has conceald all its lofty and varied beauty and sublimity— No rain has fal'n for two months— The sun rises and sets as if it threatend to pierce the earth with its ball of fire— The atmesphere is dense and impenetrable—the mountains totaly

---

[1] The 1860 edition of *Leaves of Grass*.

obscured. We shall see you some time — I want Han to see her Mother—for a change. I shall come to New York for her myself— I want to visit it— I think that I shall have to return to that place or Boston or get nearer some city— Give us more poems Walt— I hope there'l be a genearl big row—in the papers— Stir em up well— I look for it.

Charlie

I want a handsome bound volume for a *keepsake*—mind that now

Burlington June 1865

Mother Whitman

It is folly for me to write to you any more. You must come here and judge for yourself, precisely the tasks I am performing, and you may perchance also see, for yourself, the less than thanks; the contumely, and systematic disrespect I recieve for all. It is now over 3 years since Hannah has been in this condition, and I have been under the obligation to do for her, also for myself, domesticaly, and attend to my business, get a livelihood the best way I can, allmost by begging; without experiencing from her the smallest interest, sympathy or consideration for the responsibilities, cares, and endeavours that I incurr— Her sole understanding appears to be to have her own wants satisfied, even to every childish desire, and perfectly indifferent to my claims, self denials, or embarrassments. Certainly I never met with so much selfishness and imbecility; so little true pride, or sense of justice. It is whine—whine—whine on forever— slur—slur— I never make a remark but what it is met with some personality. Now you know that no two persons can possibly dwell together where one is constantly exercising either criticism or this species of vulgar wit upon the other.

Her present sickness has nothing whatever to do with it. I experienced it in Brooklyn— I might as well be a hod carrier or shoemaker, for all the difference it would make to her— She appears to take it for granted that I was constituted for the sole one purpose of drudgery—

I would not complain of the extraneous duties I perform, if met with the smallest appreciation: any sentiment whatever. But as it is I cannot but feel debased, and cannot view her with other feelings than gravest disappointment. Shall I tell you my experience this morning?

I get up at 4 O'clock, I workd in my garden until nearly 7: then I was compelld as I usualy do, to make the fire; get my own breakfast—saw wood for the morning—wash out a pitcher for milk, and finaly repair my pantaloons: this before 8 o'clock, and then go to my business—Han just then appearing, to declare her utter disrespect for me, and saying that she was glad I was going, and did not care whether she ever saw me again.

I am alone with her, which gives her the advantage over me: But I sometimes grow disgusted with her selfishness and total want of all womanly sensibility. She avows that she would not stay here an hour, if she could get to her friends: and, I frankly declare that I think her friends should share some of these trials, arising not so much from her disease, as her mean heartedness— Now I am not writing in a passion. I write deliberately. I will but ask her or you, to glance back and recall a single benefit that she has brought to me. When she was well, I endured every neglect.

It was too bad. I got my own breakfasts, as I do now. I get my own dinner also. My shirts were given to me to wear rough dried: this was the custom—only the collars and bands being irond, and my night clothes were just as they came from the line.

It is folly to argue against these facts— She allways indifferent to her own appearance, and she said that such was good enough for me: She is, to me, a melancholy failure, in every particular, of a woman. But she is a great fret— She avowd, yesterday, that she would do me all the injury she could: This is an old curse of hers. I am completely disgusted— I am content to let her have this house for a home, as long as she lives if she can do any thing, or get any person to live with her: I can sell it and make 6 or 800 dollars — It was an Irish den, allmost when I took it— I have spent 600 dollars on it and done 300 dollars personal work. I am constantly recieving congratulations on the improvement. The very Irish declare it to be wonderfull— But my exertions give me no satisfaction, and I have performd so much, from that spirit within me, which must beautify what it can: But I have faild with Han: I was faint heartd at first, still I labourd for her on true principle— I find in her no true charity, no genuine friendliness no pride in or for me; in the talent I have; or no veneration for the sacrifices I have made, the labour I have performd, or the humiliation I have sometimes sufferd: Nothing for the Endeavour of a Man: whom she lives with as her husband: who has most conscientiously studied her good, her wellfare, wants; and anticipated most of her needs.

I know that she is sick, but I cannot help it if her back snaps in two, and she dies the next minute—I think that I am entitled allmost to veneration for the services I have renderd, and the extraneous duties, clearly belonging to woman's sphere—

She remarked to a person the other day, that I had got used to things and did not mind it.

This is a fair avowal of her total imbecility— No man can become used to it: It is out of his place—To come home hungry and instead of a dinner, seize upon a stale crust or loaf, and piece of cold meat, and so grub out his life: She does not appear to have the smallest perception of any other cares, wants, wishes than her own.

Now I would not complain, I would not murmur; all that I do I would perform graciously, cheerfully, if I met with a just appreciation of these things, or any estimation of myself— of my needs— my professional aims— If I experienced in word or deed any thing from her, indicative of that congeniality or friendship so essential to domestic life; so necessary to Home:

There is one thing respecting my house; It must not be expected that it will take care of itself when I am away— Three months would behold it a wilderness, outgrown with weeds. It needs constant attention

I have 5 Grape vines started—and a vegatable and flower garden—all flourishing, as new things grow— And there are many covetous eyes on the place: The location is desirable: I could have realised 1000 dollars on it, this spring.

But I am content to let it go. It is absurd for me to work as I do merely from the love or spirit of doing. I will go West. I think that I can make much money there, and keep Han comfortable with her friends; but I do not want to return: I would rather go to Patagonia.

Han has been no wife—my feelings have been grievously smitten— I have been taunted with some things past, which she should have had too much self respect ever to have utterd, even though She never had true feeling for me—She experiences no obligation to others. When I mentioned that I was sending to you, and suggested her looking up something for Andrews little vagrants— she never even lookd for any thing.

I am glad that she has friends to rely upon, for sympathy; on her brother Walter's affection, upon George's and yourself; and I will be found reliable, practicaly, whilst I live—

You must come up, if you can, in a little while—I will send you the money — I have bought no furniture—but shall prepare another room.

There is one thing I have become used to— disappointment, Isolation. dwelling within myself; doing out of myself, without a single speculation of future recognition or further recompense.

Charlie.

This letter has been written for a long time. I have concluded to send it to you. Realy my experience robs my heart of all charity— Han has a plausible superficiality, but under that she is the devil, to me— She does me no service — I buy my shirts, and do immense drudgery— Her own things run into neglect. She will not dress herself decently, but in place of this, when I come home to dinner, (I never see her at breakfast) she manages to quarrell me out of it— so that I leave it half eaten—She begins with questioning me about my room, when she had better be reasoning upon her own short comings, and goes so far as to intimate that I have sexual intercourse with my pupils, at my room.

She is a damnd mean —reckless, characterless woman and deserves (instead of the comfortable home she has and a provident man) the poor house, or any place—neither will I put up with it— She has been a poor shirking thing allways and only does right, when intimidated

Charlie

Now I will only say further that I do not write this, hoping or expecting aught from you or her friends— I do not care what your or their opinion may be of myself—I am used to hearing that you have no respect for me, and that you burn up my letters, or dont read them— I know my own trials—one of Han phrases is, that, "She hates me with a perfect hatred" and thanks the Lord for it;" and it is the only time she calls upon the Lord's name— She will stand in the middle of the room, and defy me, whilst I am at dinner, instead of getting it on the table, and repeat, that she will question me about my room, at all times, whenever she likes, and she dont care whether it pleases me not. I will leave these facts to any decently disposed woman, or any ordinarily informd person— How long can such a woman, count on a man's forbearance.

In just one week after I shall have gone, she will scratch her head, and call herself a fool—come to the truth.

I will not live so, be so treated you may rely upon it — If there is no other way I will open my condition to my neighbour opposite, who has a mortgage on the house—and leave—and I never want to see or hear of her again—

She has treated me, meanest, beyond belief or representation

Charlie—

She is well enough now to travel or do any thing—

If it was not for the universal sympathy I recieve from the people here (in view of my industry) and the general spirit of kindliness, I would not remain here another day, but I would go and let the world have it say—my annoyances are too mean, unprovoked—It is low—low—vulgar and despicable

Burlington April 1866

Walter Whitman

Your letter to Han was recd and duly deliverd. She is I think, better than for a long time past. Only one new vargary has originated with her, and that is that I shall go away; rent the house to her, and she will take boarders; there is but one step from this to insanity—

Han has an idea that she could accomplish that for 3 or 4 persons, easily, which she has, under no circumstances, done for me, not ten times in as many years. I have just taken up a note against the property: and I think that with reasonable success I may clear it all, by next Spring. But the idea that Han runs the house and I am but the secondary drudge must be dismissd

I see but one way to bring this matter into a realizistic shape or condition, and that is, to take her at her word; "to go away" and put the place and herself under the guardianship of an attorney.

Much of this difficulty has arisen from the miserable teachings of her mother, who enjoined upon her, when we were first married not to perform these little services for me, which naturaly would suggest themselves to a kind and considerate wife, and endear her to her husband: Because I might be spoild, by it.

Mrs Whitman has been toward me, a silly old woman —for why I do not know—I never was under obligations to her for anything. If she brought a half loaf of bread to my house, she took butter or tea away in return for it, and I never had a meal at her table that I did not pay for. But Mrs Whitman never did possess a particle of honest frankness —on the contrary, in one instance, I will not her mention, a more than mean, a wicked duplicity toward myself.

Perhaps I would not look upon "Leaves of Grass" with

so much melancholy regard, if I was not experiencing a practical version of it: Irregular—disorderly: indifferent, or defiant—the lower animal instincts—no accountability. no moral sense or principle— No true, inherent, practical sympathy for anything; myself; disappointments, or endeavours. Nothing of me, or of the future to arise for me, out of my labour, and progressions.

Han has no more moral sense of marriage than an Ethiopian, of the field—Gives herself to a man and nothing more — Your letters and those of her friends shall be allways forwarded to her. I am simply disgusted with so much selfishness—

C L Heyde

There is one other change, to the last notion of Han's, and that is "She" can go "home," and cook for her mother: "her mother said so." She sometimes says that she has no friends. I believe it, since this "home" is offrd, in a menial capacity, and the service that is *imagined* can be extracted from her. *My* idea was, that, if I did go to Europe, "to let her board, in the most comfortable manner, and raise herself from ill health and drudgery—

Burlington Dec 1886

Friend Walt.

I have sent to you the "Galaxy"; It contains two articles, one on Whitman and one on Swinburne,[1]—I have read both criticisms, with great satisfaction. Richard Grant White has but paid just sympathy to a true poet "Swinburne"; The criticism is a "Poem," in itself. It has the comprehensiveness, and the fearless recognition of the divine

---

[1] The *Galaxy* for Dec. 1, 1866, contained an article by John Burroughs, "Walt Whitman and His 'Drum Taps' " (II, 606-615) and a review of Swinburne by Richard Grant White (II, 665-670).

idea, or sentiment of "Love," as expressd by the Poet, he writes upon—Swinburne electrifies me. I read one verse of his "Laus Veneris," in a store, and bought the book— When critics or ordinary readers, or writers scribble him down, the Sun will cease to procreate and vitalize the earth. He is cultivated, and "passion" is his subject— "St Doro-thy" is saddening, and the "Leper" oh how passionately full of piteous Love—and the "Orchard" oh! the night is all starrd by it, and earth burdend with dewy fragrancies—

There is enough beauty in your "Leaves" to make a rare book, and not cast out sensuous extravagance either. But you are wonderfully, woefully mistaken in the privileage you take of being merely savagely material, and consequently offensively vulgar— Han is much better than usual, and is continualy promising to write to her Mother.

C L Heyde

Burlington   Mar 1867

Dear Mother Whitman

I believe that I have at last provoked Han to write you a letter: I think that she sent one to the Post Office, a few days since, by one of the neighbours children— Well, we must consider Han charitably, for she appears to be un-able to perform certain things promptly, or systematicaly. I get very much out of patience; matters have a most sloven-ly look, yet she drudges hard too — She is quite stout bodied, yet complains of her back.

I wrote a long letter to you last winter, but I discovered that I had not directed it correctly, so it may be you did not recieve it— It was directed (208 Box) instead of 218—

Spring is coming fast, and I am considering about the garden: Painting has been very dull— My house would bring $3000— I could rent it for 275 dollars. Han re-

cieves letters from Walter pretty often —He sent his
photograph lately which now adorns the "what-not"—
(rather dusty) It has a very matter of fact, bluff, old gentleman look—

I keep pretty well—

Yours Sincerely
C L Heyde

Burlington   Dec 1868

Dear Mother Whitman

Hannah's thumb was amputated, yesterday, (Tuesday)
by Dr Thayer, assisted by his son. I was present, of course.
She was under the influence of ether, and did not experience
any pain. It is the left hand, and the entire thumb was taken
off. It had been dead, at the extremity for many days, but
the doctor allowed it the longest time advisable (as it was
quite offensive) and she was constantly breathing the effluvia
from it. It was a very unhappy sight, to see the operation:
she is only tolerable, this morning, but I am now in hopes,
that she will recover quickly; allthough her nervous system
is much prostrated, by this second trial. The opinion is
however, that she will be rather feeble, all winter.

If she could once compose herself to quietude. But,
even in her miserable state, she must worry — try to sew,
and rip up old dresses. She must be more carefull.

I have nothing to withdraw about Walter. When Han
was sick, at Bellows Falls, he wrote a most ridiculous letter
to her, when she was not able to hear it read to her. And
he was well advised about her condition. Mr. Shurtleffe
was much surprised at it;   There was nothing tangible
about it, or was it in any manner comforting, for there was
nothing beyond what some folorn spiritualist would have
vritten, under the moonshine.—

It is not necessary for you to even think of coming here, at your age — Hannah is well taken care of, and has every want, and wish gratified

I have no desire to annoy, or give you unnecessary concern — I could have stated mere facts, without so much detail, but I was moved, by my situation to relate every thing, precisely as it was. Besides Han's illness, I was exceedingly annoyd, at the unnecessary, miserable condition of our domestic affairs —

Yours respectfully
and kindly
C L Heyde —

Burlington   June 13   70

Walter Whitman

Han has received all your letters, also the Radical, containing a very complimentary testimony by a genuine woman, to your "Leaves of Grass"[1]: Yet you percieve, even the praise she bestows is qualified with the general recoil, which all natures of true human sensibility experience, at your (mistaken) barbarism. The louse and the maggot know as much about procreation as you do, and when you unveil and denude yourself you descend to the level of the dog, with the bitch, merely. But I intended to write of Han only. She is tolerably well. The swelling in her neck has subsided. She makes a half barbarous life for herself, however and allmost baffles all my efforts at times to humanize her. I have come to view her as a being, half child, with small promptings to her social obligations, and no longer hold her accountable for her ways— Somethings she does very well, but her speech is so vagrant, that, to use

---

[1] Anne Gilchrist, "A Woman's Estimate of Walt Whitman," published anonymously in the *Radical*, VII, 345-359 (May, 1870), and reprinted in *In Re Walt Whitman* (Philadelphia, 1893).

her own expression, "I must not put any meaning in her words."

Her usual supiness, or sluggishness continues. I think it must be in the blood. It is very trying to me—Respecting her neglect in not writing to her mother, it is simply the want of inclination, but she treats her good, kind neighbours, who came and watched over her, during her last dreadfull sickness, the same way. On her recovery she never crossed the street to thank them. I need scarcely explain to you what gratitude is: Han could have done better and saved me great mortification, but her mother in Brooklyn, thwarted my endeavours, by continualy rushing in, and without sufficient occasion, advising seperation. Oh! such stupid recklessness and wickedness. The Allmighty it seems to me, has no gift, in the Future to amend the unnecessary and degrading experience I have endured—nor would I enter upon such a life again, after it, were a thousand years of mortal existence promised to me (to follow) every year to enter upon a different phase of life, each growing brighter and happier than the last, still ascending upon a greater scale of grandeur and felicity.

But Han is to remain as she is and where she is. It is imperative: any positive pressure socialy, or change might prove disastrous. She is looking well, but is never feeling well—has head aches or something— She treats herself too barbarously entirely.

Mrs. Whitman rather intimates a desire to make Han another visit: She is becoming too aged—and it is as much as Han can do to take care of herself. For my part I have as much care as I desire, and more than I ever anticipated— I have just paid off the mortgage on my house and have sustained myself here, not so much upon the merit or appreciation of my paintings, as by a certain force of character, which has found sympathy among the people.

Yours truly   C L Heyde

Burlington [February?] 5 1873

Dear Mother Whitman.

Han has recieved your letter. We were informed of Walters affliction,[1] and supposed it to be much worse than you represent.

I wrote to George, immediately, which was nearly a week ago, requesting him to inform us of Walters condition, precisely, but recieved no reply.

I have since directed a letter to Washington, supposing George might be there, as the papers represented Walter to be quite low—

Han has written to you some time ago— We are grieved to learn that Mrs Whitmans[2] health does not improve—but feel gratefull that Walter's condition is not so serious. Han is but tolerable well— We have had a rigorous winter: I am well, but feel very much out of sorts with the precarious state of my worldly affairs. I am sincerely gratefull for your box of—every thing, dainty—pretty and needfull for Han—   C L Heyde

Burlington Vermont.
Feb 27. 1885.

Bro Walt.

Han grows stronger daily: relishes her food, and consumes as much as she used when well: Yet she has very bad spells, which she rather encourages: This however is constitutional, and for which, her good old deceased friend,

---

[1] A stroke of paralysis.
[2] Jeff's wife, Martha, was i'l with tuberculosis, which caused her death on Feb. 19, 1873.

Dr S. P. Thayer, pronounced, irremedial, by medicine—
Mr Heyde, he used to say, We know of no medicine that
can cure it: still he allways sympathised her, kindly, tenderly,
and declared her to be, physicaly a perfect woman.

She has omitted taking bromide, now, for 8 nights. If
she could be persuade to desisted from rubbing a most per-
nicious coloring ointment, into her scalp, with an old tooth
brush, her improvement would be greater. She denied the
practice, but I have observed, from behind her chair, a complete scab allmost, or the blood starting from the irritation:

Christ, O! Christ! It makes me religious, and dis-
couraged with women. Why gray hair is fashionable: and
then cork screw curls, drawn over her forehead to cover
wrinkles.

C L H

June 89

Bro Walt. Your letter to Han, with 1 dollar—recieved—
She is very nervous: did not sleep all night. I have a roost
in noreast corner—small room, rough but brightens with
early morning light. 4 or 5 Oclock—

I get solitary breakfast—best I can—allways did—dont
mind it, if I can be helpd a little at times— sell paintings,
trifle over cost of framing—go with poor clothing—very
seedy—dont mind that can I but keep square on provisions
—no let bill double on me— You have great enthusaism
to aid and help you perhaps with money— No such sentiment here. I painted Vermont State Coat of Arms 26 years
ago—now Executive Seal—got 50 dollars for it — This is
sculptured on the Gettysburg Monument, and other Army
Associations— Got all things acknowledged by G. G. Ben-
edict in daily Journall, amounts to nothing toward selling
paintings Oh State pride—Edmunds and J. Steuart—

complain of poverty   miserable people—ye grand country
in Scenery— Speak to George— I must keep the house and
mantain it— Han must have a home— She could survive
a sale or removal— I wrote to Geoge before Christmas
advising him to send money— This box amonts to nothing
—better had sent the dollar it cost to forward it— Han has
used some thread out of it— the handsome bed spread, was
examined, then thrust back in the box, and pushed uneder
a table—getting dusty and musty — I have not a comfortable bed for years—yet I can sleep, after a can crowd
in a form, and draw covering over me—warm with an old
overcoat and cotton coverlid— I have a blanket now— I
dont require it — I never undressed coldest nights last
winter—tired oft as an old vetrans, I dropped in my tracks,
Yes and slept, after a hard days battle with life— Oh! oh!
what an experience—narative. Got a heater last winter,
gave a picture for it—pipe passing into chimney through
my room mad it comfortable—
My Sister on Staten Island has been dangerously ill for
some weeks—now convalescing—a frail looking creature,
and yet the mother of Several children, and grand children—
sincere guiless—beloved— — I have not seen either of
my Sisters, in 35 years. I have numerous choice painting,
I reserve for an appreciative, customer perhaps— Fine it
is said— God, it is hard   Charlie.

                                        April 7, 1890
Bro Walt.
    Good Kind Friend— Your letter, enclosing $2— most
gratefully recieved. I assure you. How you help us
along— How could we ever survive, but for your good-
ness—
    Han is but poorly as yet. A beautifull day overhead, and
an adventurous robin chirping at 4 O'clock this morning—

I heard him from my window—but cold chilly, freezing nights prevail— I am quite unsteady on my legs, from effects of the grippe—and my stomach is weak, but I feel stronger this morning and encouraged—

God bless you Walt, he has qualified you all through your life, with a benevolent disposity, and a sustaining philosophy—

Han talks of you nearly all the time— She can now promenade on the back piaza where you may remember the sun used to fall so benignly— —

Dear Friend
Gratefull yours ever
Charlie

[November, 1890]

Studio, over Kitchen—fair day—windy however—lake rough—blustering. Han below doing domestic service— very much better in health—stronger, nervous somewhat— yet doing wonders—after her year of sore trial—

Recieved your imprint,[1] or wonderfull compilation on classicaly poetic emanations of celebrities in times past, of all degrees—. How true you note, that time composes, completes the understanding, qualifies the decree, as it were, finaly, justly of degrees, consumate excellence, superiority—

Yourself now Eminent—a judge. You should have a liberal emolument, or price for this last, most complete production— I feel assured you will— I remember Bryant; You once brought him to my studio in Brooklyn— I can imagine or recall him now, as he sat on the extreme end of my lounge — High Priest of Nature! Thanatopsis—! Durand essayd to color the theme from his rather weak (never vain palette). A failure. The grand old rocks, an-

---

[1] An offprint of Whitman's essay "Old Poets," which appeared in the *North American Review*, CLI, 610-614 (Nov., 1890).

cient as the sun! Very new rocks" wrote one critic— Cole
might, could have portrayd it, with his dramatic power!²

And now Walt— I am moved practicaly, for ourselves,
lifes subsistence—our homestead for many years—consecrat-
ed in an measure by good mother Whitmans presence, years
ago, for a brief so-journ—and by Yours— —well known —
Due on taxes yet 10 dollars— 1 years interst—15 dollars—

Charlie

² Asher Brown Durand (1796-1886) and Thomas Cole (1801-1848)
were prominent New York artists, both interested, like their friend Bryant,
in the American landscape. Durand painted a picture entitled "Thanatopsis,"
to which Heyde refers.

Appendix

Phrenological Analysis
of the Character of Whitman

Trent Collection catalogue, page 66, number 24. Although portions of the phrenological diagnosis of Whitman, made in the summer of 1849 by Lorenzo N. Fowler, have been several times published by the poet and by others and a valuable study dealing with "Walt Whitman and His Chart of Bumps" has been made by Edward Hungerford,[1] the entire analysis seems heretofore never to have appeared in print.

The first part of the manuscript is in the hand of a clerk or professional copyist, who wrote it out presumably at the direction of Fowler himself; the second part is a transcript of the phrenologist's estimate of the size of Whitman's "bumps" made in pencil by Dr. R. M. Bucke. In order to understand the significance of the numerals the reader is informed that 1 means "very small," 2 "small," 3 "moderate," 4 "average," 5 "full," 6 "large," 7 "very large." The first part represents Fowler's conclusions based upon the measurements of the poet's head and is in many respects a remarkably penetrating character sketch. After a reading of it one may more easily understand why Whitman chose to celebrate himself as a representative of humanity.

Phrenological Description

of

W. (Age 29 / Occupation Printer) Whitman

by

L. N. Fowler N. York July 16—1849.

[1] *American Literature*, II, 350-384 (Jan., 1931).

You were blessed by nature with a good constitution and power to live to a good old age. You were undoubtedly descended from a long-lived family. You were not (like many) prematurely developed—did not get ripe like a hot house-plant but you can last long and grow better as you grow older if you are careful to obey the laws of health, of life and of mental and physical development. You have a large sized brain giving you much mentality as a whole. You are well calculated to enjoy social life— Few men have *all* the social feelings as strong as you have. Your love and regard for woman as such are strong and you are for elevating and ameliorating the female character. You were inclined to marry at an early age. You could not well bear to be deprived of you domestic privileges and enjoyments. You are very fond of children or pets and would much desire to have your *own* intelligent and respected. You are also very fond of home and think much of having one of your own and of making it comfortable and attractive. You would like to travel and yet to go and leave family and friends would be a *task*. You are one of the most friendly men in the world and your happiness is greatly depending on your social relations. You are familiar and open in your intercourse with others but you do not by so doing lose your dignity. You would be or *are* a kind husband—an affectionate father. and a sincere friend and a feeling obliging neighbor. You can easily pass from one thing to another and you prefer short comprehensive speeches to long yarns about nothing. You have much energy when you are aroused but you are not easily moved at trifles. You would if obliged to, fight bravely for friends, woman, moral character, children and honor. You choose to fight with tongue and pen rather than with your fist. You are not quarrelsome but You mind your own business and like to see others do the same. You are cautious and look well to the future. to consequences and obstructions and are generally pretty sure you are right before you "go ahead." Your courage is probably more *moral* than *physical*. Your appetite is most *too* strong naturally and your food relishes well. You are pretty well calculated to *resist* disease and to soon *recover* if you are attacked. by it. You are no hypocrite but are plain spoken and are what you *appear* to be at all times. You are in fact most *too* open at times and have not alway enough restraint in speech. You are more careful about what you *do* than you are about what you say— You are independent, not wishing to be a slave yourself or to enslave others. You have your own opinions and think for yourself. You wish to work on your own hook, and are inclined to take the lead. You are very firm in general and not easily driven from your position. Your sense of justice, of right and wrong is strong and you can see much that is unjust and inhuman in the present condition of society. You are but little inclined to the spiritual or devotional and have but little regard for creeds or ceremonies. You are not any too sanguine and generally realize as much as you hope for— You are very sympathetic and easily moved by suffering. and take much interest in those movements that are of a reformatory and philanthropic character. You are not any too fond of property but value it as a *means* —are not a penny-man, and despise narrowminded penuriousness—You have taste and considerable imagination but it does not blind you to fact or reality. You can adapt yourself to time place and company but you do not try to act out another's character but are yourself at all times. You have both reason and perception. and hence can reason well. You have a strong desire to see everything and your knowledge is practical and *available*. You have a good mechanical eye and can judge well of and reccollect forms and proportions well. You have a good sense of order either *mentally* or *physically*. By practice might make a good accountant. You can locate well and have a taste for geography. You are a great reader and have a good memory of facts and events much better than their *time*. You can compare. illustrate. discriminate. and criticise with much ability. You can be sarcastic if you choose. You are a good physiognomist. You have a good command of language especially if excited

Size of brain	6	Benevolence	6 to 7
Strength of System	6	Constructiveness	5
Degree of activity	5	Ideality	5 to 6
Propelling or executive		Sublimity	5 to 6
faculties	6	Imitation	5
Vital Temperament	5	Mirthfulness	5
Motive apparatus	6	Intellectual faculties	5 to 6
Mental apparatus	5	Observing and Knowing	
Amativeness	6	faculties	6
Philoprogenitiveness	6 to 7	Individuality	6
Adhesiveness	6	Form	6
Inhabitiveness	6	Size	6
Concentrativeness	4	Weight	5
Combativeness	6	Color	3
Destructiveness	5 to 6	Order	5+
Alimentiveness	6	Calculation	5
Acquisitiveness	4	Locality	6
Secretiveness	3	Eventuality	6
Cautiousness	6	Time	3
Approbativeness	4	Tune	4
Self Esteem	6 to 7	Language	5
Firmness	6	Causality	5
Conscientiousness	6	Comparison	6
Hope	4	Suavitiveness	4
Marvellousness	3	Intuition of human nature	6
Veneration	4		

List of Abbreviated Titles

Barrus   Clara Barrus. *Whitman and Burroughs, Comrades,* Boston and New York, 1931.

Bucke   Richard Maurice Bucke. *Walt Whitman,* Philadelphia, 1883.

Calamus   *Calamus, A Series of Letters Written During the Years 1868-1880 by Walt Whitman to a Young Friend (Peter Doyle).* Edited by Richard Maurice Bucke, Boston, 1897.

Camden   *The Complete Writings of Walt Whitman.* Edited by Richard Maurice Bucke, Thomas B. Harned, and Horace L. Traubel, New York [1902]. Vols. I-X.

Donaldson   Thomas Donaldson. *Walt Whitman, The Man,* New York, 1896.

Furness   Clifton Joseph Furness. *Walt Whitman's Workshop,* Cambridge, Mass., 1928.

Glicksberg   Charles I. Glicksberg. *Walt Whitman and the Civil War,* Philadelphia, 1933.

Inclusive   *Leaves of Grass by Walt Whitman. Inclusive Edition.* Edited by Emory Holloway, Garden City, N. Y., 1926.

Kennedy   William Sloane Kennedy. *Reminiscences of Walt Whitman,* Paisley, 1896.

Perry   Bliss Perry. *Walt Whitman, His Life and Work,* Boston and New York, 1906.

Traubel   Horace L. Traubel. *With Walt Whitman in Camden,* New York, 1908-1914. Vols. I-III.

Uncollected *The Uncollected Poetry and Prose of Walt Whitman.* Edited by Emory Holloway, Garden City, N. Y., 1921. Vols. I-II.

Index